Active Ageing with Music

IOEPress

Active Ageing with Music

Supporting wellbeing in the Third and Fourth Ages

Andrea Creech, Susan Hallam, Maria Varvarigou, and Hilary McQueen

Institute of Education Press

First published in 2014 by the Institute of Education, University of London,
20 Bedford Way, London WC1H 0AL
ioepress.co.uk

British Library Cataloguing in Publication Data:
A catalogue record for this publication is available from the British Library

ISBNs
978-1-78277-029-9 (paperback)
978-1-78277-089-3 (PDF eBook)
978-1-78277-090-9 (ePub eBook)
978-1-78277-091-6 (Kindle eBook)

Typeset by Quadrant Infotech (India) Pvt Ltd
Printed by CPI Group (UK) Ltd, Croydon CR0 4YY

Cover images: choir ©iStock.com/McIninch; piano lesson ©Thinkstock.com/AlbertD; band ©iStock.com/Alija

Contents

List of figures and tables

Acknowledgements

The authors gratefully acknowledge the UK Research Councils' New Dynamics of Ageing Programme, the funder of the Music for Life Project.

The authors would also like to thank all of the participants in the Music for Life Project, acknowledging the fellowship, time, and thoughtful contributions shared by the older people, facilitators and support staff at all of the Music for Life Project research sites.

Notes on contributors

Dr Andrea Creech is Reader in Education at the Institute of Education, University of London. Following an international orchestral career Andrea was director of a Community Music School, developing programmes for learners of all ages. Since completing her PhD in Psychology in Music Education, Andrea has been Co-Director for several funded research projects relating to musical engagement across the lifespan, including a major research programme that focused on the role of music in supporting social, emotional, and cognitive wellbeing amongst older people. Andrea has presented at international conferences and published widely on topics concerned with ageing well, musical development, and lifelong learning in music. She is a Board member of the International Society for Music Education and is on several editorial boards for international journals. In addition Andrea is a Fellow of the Higher Education Academy, Secretary for the Education Section of the British Psychological Society and a member of the Society for Education, Music and Psychology Research.

Dr Susan Hallam is Professor of Education and Music Psychology at the Institute of Education, University of London. She pursued careers as both a professional musician and a music educator before completing her psychology studies and becoming an academic in 1991. Her research interests include disaffection from school, ability grouping and homework and issues relating to learning in music, practising, performing, musical ability, musical understanding, and the effects of music on behaviour and studying. She is the author of numerous books including *Instrumental Teaching: A Practical Guide to Better Teaching and Learning* (1998), *The Power of Music* (2001), *Music Psychology in Education* (2005), and *Preparing for success: a practical guide for young musicians* (2012); editor of *The Oxford Handbook of Psychology of Music* (2009) and *Music Education in the 21st Century in the United Kingdom: Achievements, analysis and aspirations* (2010); and has extensive other scholarly contributions. She is past editor of *Psychology of Music, Psychology of Education Review,* and *Learning Matters.* She has twice been Chair of the Education Section of the British Psychological Society and is an Academician of the Learned Societies for the Social Sciences.

Dr Hilary McQueen studied music and subsequently psychology and education. She is currently a tutor on the post-compulsory Initial Teacher Education programmes at the Institute of Education, University of London. In addition to a number of articles and chapters about teaching and learning, she co-authored *Key Concepts in Philosophy* (2010) with one of her sons, Paddy. Her book *Roles, Rights and Responsibilities in UK Education: Tensions and inequalities* is in preparation for the Palgrave Pivot series. Her research interests include the development of effective learners. She is also a private music teacher, accompanist, and occasional composer.

Dr Maria Varvarigou is a Lecturer in Music and Performing Arts at Canterbury Christ Church University, a Senior Researcher at the Sidney de Haan Centre for Arts and Health and a Visiting Research Associate at the Institute of Education, University of London. Maria has been performing as a solo singer, oboist, and chorister for many years. She has participated in several recordings of Greek traditional songs and has developed a great interest in performance practices of traditional music. She completed her PhD in 2009 as a scholar of the A.S. Onassis Foundation. She is a Fellow of the Royal Society for the Encouragement of Arts, Manufactures and Commerce (RSA) and a Fellow of the Higher Education Academy. Her special areas of interest include music, health, and wellbeing; intergenerational music-making; vernacular performance practices; choral conducting education, primary music education, and effective teaching and learning in higher and professional education.

Preface

This book advocates the view that active music-making may have a significant positive influence on the quality of life amongst older people. The focus is on research concerned with group music-making within social contexts, where aspects of 'wellbeing', 'active ageing', or 'quality of life' have been reported as positive outcomes. We draw upon a growing body of innovative international research concerned with the social, emotional, and cognitive benefits of community music-making amongst older adults and representing a range of contexts and ways of making music. Key messages from that body of research are illustrated with personal stories from participants in the Music for Life Research Project (Hallam *et al.*, 2011), funded by the UK Research Councils' 'New Dynamics of Ageing' programme.

Active Ageing with Music is a resource for academics working in the fields of music education or psychology of music and for music practitioners who are interested in leading musical activities with older people. Most importantly, this book will be of interest to individual older adults who are interested in how they may preserve and sustain their cognitive, social, and emotional wellbeing throughout the latter stages of their lives.

The New Dynamics of Ageing Programme

The New Dynamics of Ageing (NDA) Programme was a major eight-year, interdisciplinary research initiative in the UK. The programme involved collaboration amongst the five UK Research Councils (Economic and Social Research Council, Engineering and Physical Sciences Research Council, Biotechnology and Biological Sciences Research Council, Medical Research Council, and Arts and Humanities Research Council). An overarching aim that united all of the NDA projects was to increase understanding of the forces that drive ageing and the responses to ageing that could achieve maximum benefits for older people (NDA, 2013).

During the final phase of the NDA programme, the Music for Life Project was funded, alongside eight other Arts and Humanities research projects concerned with, for example, depictions of ageing in fiction, representations of ageing in visual art, and the place of theatre in representations and recollections of ageing.

The Music for Life Project

The Music for Life Project focused on creative and participative musical activities in the lives of older people, exploring potential links between music-making and social, emotional, and cognitive wellbeing. We were particularly interested in the processes that underpinned some of the positive benefits of music-making that had been reported in previous research.

Three case study sites in England acted as partners in the research: The Sage, Gateshead; Westminster Adult Education Service; and the Connect programme at the Guildhall School of Music & Drama. Collectively, the musical activities at these three sites included singing in small and large groups, rock groups, and classes for guitar, ukulele, steel pans, percussion, recorder, music appreciation, and keyboard. A control (comparison) group was made up of individuals attending language classes (four groups); art/craft classes (five groups); yoga; social support (two groups); a book group; and a social club.

The Sage Gateshead

The Silver Programme at the Sage Gateshead aims to develop the broadest possible range of musical opportunities for people over the age of 50, by providing a programme of supported daytime music workshops and events in a structured, relaxed, and enjoyable atmosphere. The programme provides opportunities for participants to revive past musical skills, as well as encouraging and developing new and emerging ones, enhancing musical abilities, and encouraging positive mental and physical heath. Participants have the opportunity to perform regularly in public concerts. The weekly Silver Programme actively involves up to a thousand people aged 50 and over in an eclectic spread of music activities including singing of many kinds, steel pans, guitars, recorder, folk ensemble, music theory, and samba.

The Connect Programme of the Guildhall School of Music and Drama

The Guildhall School of Music and Drama Connect Programme runs community projects with people of all ages in East London. 'Connect' music projects are distinctive in that their focus is on activities where participants create and perform music together, linking story-telling and reminiscing to creative music-making. The programmes run by Connect to date have largely focused on young people. For the Music for Life Project the musical activities with older people took place in the community rooms of sheltered housing (assisted living) accommodation in East London. These musical activities included intergenerational music sessions involving the older people making music together with children from local primary schools (see Chapter 7).

The Westminster Adult Education Service

Westminster Adult Education Service (WAES) music department (London) runs a wide range of musical programmes catering for students at all levels of expertise. Courses are offered in a range of musical genres, specializing in singing, playing instruments, sound engineering and using sequencers, music theory, and composing. Learners over the age of 50 are strongly represented across the music curriculum. In 2010–11 older learners participated in courses as diverse as music technology, radio production, piano, music theory, guitar, and ukulele. The WAES music department is distinctive in that it operates satellite centres in residential care homes where older people participate in choir and music-appreciation classes.

Control group

Control (comparison) groups were recruited to take part in the Music for Life Project, comprising adults involved in social activities other than music. These included individuals attending language classes (four groups); art/craft classes (five groups); yoga; social support (two groups); a book group; and a social club. All of the groups apart from the book group were based in the London area; the book group was based in a rural area of England.

Methods

A multi-methods approach to data collection was taken, incorporating both qualitative and quantitative elements. The methods included:

- questionnaires for participants (music and comparison groups)
- focus-group interviews with music participants
- individual semi-structured interviews with music participants
- questionnaires for facilitators
- individual semi-structured interviews with facilitators
- videos and observations of teaching/rehearsal sessions
- videos and observations of performances
- email interviews with area coordinators of Age UK
- interviews with family, friends, care-givers
- consultative conference for stakeholders.

Questionnaires for participants

The questionnaires for participants comprised two psychological-needs scales related to wellbeing (see Chapter 1 for theoretical background to these scales). In addition, the questionnaires asked participants to provide demographic information and to respond to questions about past participation in group activities, the activity (or activities) that they were currently taking part in, what encouraged them to join, and the benefits as well as the barriers to participation. Those participating in the music activities completed questionnaires in September–October 2009 and again in July–September 2010, after several months of music-making.

Questionnaires for facilitators

The facilitators' questionnaire asked about their qualifications and experience, reasons for involvement, benefits and difficulties or challenges of leading groups at their centre, if and how they adapted their activity for older learners, and their views on reasons for and possible barriers to participation. Two scales were included: the first assessed facilitators' views of successful leadership derived from the work of Hallam (1998; 2006b). The second was the Basic Needs Satisfaction at Work scale (Deci and Ryan, 2010).

Focus-group interviews

The issues discussed in the focus-group interviews related to what it felt like being a member of the group, what were the valued aspects of participation, and what would participants like to change in order for the programmes to be more enjoyable. Issues relating to access, quality, and the benefits to the wider community were also explored.

Individual semi-structured interviews

Semi-structured interviews with the older people who participated in groups focused on the individuals' involvement in either music or other groups, their musical preferences, their experiences from participating in the activities, their perception of what makes a 'good leader' of musical (or other) activities, their thoughts on the role of musical activities in their local communities, and possible connections between music participation and wellbeing.

Interviews with facilitators provided a deeper understanding of their musical backgrounds, training, skills required, and issues relating to working with older people. Facilitators were also asked about the benefits and challenges of leading groups, and about criteria for choice of repertoire.

Email interviews

A set of email questions covering local music provision and access issues was also devised for housing-scheme managers and representatives from charitable organizations, working with older people.

Observations

A range of musical activities was observed. For this purpose an observation sheet was drawn up that aimed to capture the physical arrangement of the room and content of the session. Digital recordings were made at various points in the session, for later analysis. Recordings were also made of participant performances on each of the sites.

Consultative conference

Preliminary findings were presented to over one hundred key stakeholders (representatives from agencies supporting older people and from arts organizations working with older people or interested in implementing this work), on 22 October 2010. The assembled stakeholders participated in two consultative activities, contributing their responses to the research findings, issues arising, and suggestions for ways forward. These responses were collated and analysed thematically.

Data analysis

The qualitative data derived from the questionnaires, interviews, focus groups and email communications were coded thematically, using a qualitative data analysis software tool (NVivo). A number of themes emerged that provided greater insight into aspects of leading and taking part in activities for the over 50s, including benefits and challenges for all concerned, as well as issues relating to quality, access, and inclusion. Qualitative themes were explored that related to whether there was something particularly different or special that could be derived from musical activities, as compared with other activities.

The quantitative data collected in the questionnaires were analysed using SPSS (Statistical Package for the Social Sciences). The individual items for the various scales (wellbeing, quality of life, perceptions of effective leaders, musical preferences) used in the study were summed to create the appropriate sub-elements. Statistical techniques adopted to analyse the data included basic descriptive statistics, comparisons of groups, and principal components analyses (see Chapter 1; Creech *et al.*, 2013b; Hallam *et al.*, 2013; Hallam *et al.*, 2012).

Characteristics of the participants in the Music for Life Project

A total of 500 older people took part in the study, including 398 (80 per cent) who were involved in musical groups and 102 (20 per cent) who participated in other kinds of activities such as language groups, book groups, yoga, and social clubs. Amongst both groups (music and comparison groups) the sample was predominantly female (approximately 80 per cent).

The participants in both the music and non-music activities were over the age of 50, with the exception of one of the choirs and the language groups in the WAES programme that were open to all adults. Participants in the activities were born between 1916 and 1967. The eldest was 93 and the youngest 43. Some participants did not give their age and just three participants were younger than 50. The modal age (the age appearing most often) was 65 when the data were first collected. Of those participating in the music groups, 246 (73 per cent) were aged 50–75 years, while 92 (23 per cent) were aged over 75. Of those participating in the non-musical activities 62 (75 per cent) were aged 50–75 and 21 (21 per cent) aged over 75.

There were no statistically significant differences in socio-economic status between the groups (this was calculated using postcode addresses as well as previous occupations). In both groups there was a preponderance of those in professional occupations, although in the non-music group there was a greater proportion of those who classed themselves as housewife/retired (see Table 0.1).

Table 0.1: Previous occupations* of the participants

	Music groups		Comparison groups	
Managers, directors, senior officials	10	3%	6	10%
Professional occupations	179	54%	22	38%
Associate professional and technical occupations	22	7%	8	14%
Administration and secretarial	54	16%	5	8%
Skilled trades	7	2%	3	5%
Caring, leisure and other service occupations	24	7%	2	3%
Sales and customer service	14	4%	2	3%
Process, plant and machine operatives	8	3%	0	0%
Elementary occupations	3	1%	0	0%

Housewife/retired	9	3%	11	19%
Total	330	100	59	100
Information not supplied	68		43	

*Standard Occupational Classification 2010, Office for National Statistics (ONS, 2010).

Prior musical experiences of the participants

Those who were participating in the comparison groups (not music) were asked if music was important to them. Thirty-seven individuals responded to this question. Of these five said it had never been important (14 per cent), 20 indicated that they enjoyed music from time to time (54 per cent), while 12 said that it played a central role in their lives (32 per cent).

Amongst participants in the music group, 74 per cent indicated that they had been involved in musical activities prior to the research (the large majority being choirs or singing groups), while 26 per cent were 'novices', with no prior experience of music.

Those participating in the music groups were asked about the instruments that they played. One hundred and fifty-nine participants said they played a musical instrument and 55 said they played more than one instrument. Of the instrumentalists, 82 (52 per cent) played the piano, 25 played the ukulele (16 per cent), and 23 played guitar (14 per cent). Smaller numbers of participants played the recorder, drums, violin, steel pans/drums, flute, trumpet, bass, folk instruments, or pan pipes.

Self-assessment of musical skills and knowledge

When asked to assess the level attained in their best instrument as an adult, 29 per cent of those who played instruments classified themselves as beginners, while 40 per cent considered themselves as average, 28 per cent as good, and 4 per cent as very good.

Sixty-eight of those participating in the musical groups (17 per cent of the 398 music participants) had taken graded examinations. Fifty-nine of these people indicated the level they had attained; 42 had attained up to Grade 5, 13 had attained up to Grade 8, and four had attained beyond Grade 8 level.

Sixty per cent of the music-makers (238 individuals) indicated that they could read musical notation. Of these, 105 indicated that their level of competency was 'basic', 67 indicated that it was average, 48 were 'good', and 18 were 'very good'.

Musical preferences

Participants in the musical activities were asked to indicate their preferences relating to a range of musical genres, rating different genres on a preference scale from 1 (lowest) to 10 (highest). Table 0.2 demonstrates that amongst this sample the highest rating was given to classical music ($\underline{M}$ = 7.89), while the lowest rating was assigned to electronic music ($\underline{M}$ = 2.20).

Table 0.2: Musical preferences of participants in musical activities

	Mean**	SD*
Classical	7.89	2.33
Easy listening	6.64	2.69
Blues and gospel	6.09	2.65
World and folk	5.95	2.69
Rock and pop	5.79	3.04
Country	5.71	2.84
Soundtracks	5.63	2.68
Jazz	5.40	2.83
R&B and soul	5.19	2.80
Reggae	3.29	2.52
Electronic	2.83	2.13

*SD (standard deviation) indicates the variability in the responses. Higher numbers indicate a greater range of responses.
**1 = least preferred; 10 = most preferred.

Other activities of those participating in the musical activities

Those who were participating in the musical activities also had other interests. The most common activity (45 per cent) related to some kind of physical activity, including dancing, walking, rambling, a sport, or yoga. The next most common groups of activities were arts and crafts and church-related activities (7 per cent, in each case).

Music in everyday life

Participants engaged in the musical activities were asked to indicate what role making music and listening to music played in their daily lives. Of those who responded, 26 per cent said that they often practised at home, while 42 per cent never did so. Eighty per cent reported that they sometimes or often sang at home, while 20 per cent said that they either never sang at home, or not often. Over 90 per cent indicated that playing or singing with others was something they did sometimes or often. A large majority of the sample indicated that they listened to recorded or live music, sometimes or often.

Characteristics of the facilitators

Questionnaires were completed by 14 music facilitators and eight non-music facilitators. Five respondents were male and 17 female. Of the music facilitators four were male, and 10 female. In the non-music groups only one facilitator was male. All but two were white and most were British. Overall, six had a teaching qualification. Of the musicians, seven had a Masters Degree level qualification, three had a music Diploma, and one had an 'A Level' (secondary-school diploma) qualification. The facilitators played a range of instruments, with the most popular being piano, voice, guitar, and percussion. The facilitators were asked to rate their level of expertise on their instruments. Eight of the facilitators rated themselves as 'advanced' on their first instrument, compared with one 'very good' and five 'good'.

Summary

In this preface we have described the Music for Life Project and outlined the key characteristics of the participants and the facilitators who took part. Those participating in the musical groups exhibited a range of musical expertise from beginner to those who described themselves as very good and played a wide variety of instruments, although the musical activities that they undertook largely involved singing. The facilitators were also characterized as having a wide range of skills.

Throughout *Active Ageing with Music*, examples from the Music for Life Project are used to illustrate the power of music in the lives of older people. We also draw upon the reports of excellent research concerned with this topic, from around the world. Our overarching message is that participation in music has the potential to enhance the quality of life and wellbeing of older people, contributing to sustained active ageing.

Chapter 1

Introduction

Overview

This book explores the powerful potential for music-making to support wellbeing and quality of life[1] amongst older people. We tell the story of how active engagement in music-making has been found to support cognitive, social, and emotional wellbeing in older age. The processes that underpin music's relationship with wellbeing will also be explored, focusing on contexts for learning, musical development, approaches to facilitation, and barriers to participation. Older people's own individual accounts are framed by theoretical perspectives and empirical evidence relating to how engagement with music may help individuals to respond to the challenges of growing old and experience sustained, active ageing throughout the latter life stages.

Throughout *Active Ageing with Music* we illustrate our key messages with voices of older people themselves – 'real life' stories, drawn from the findings from the 'Music for Life Project', funded by the UK Research Councils' New Dynamics of Ageing Programme and carried out between 2009 and 2012 (see Preface for details). Older people spoke of how music-making had provided a sense of purpose and structure in daily life, as well as fun and enjoyment. Belonging to a musical group was particularly powerful, generating a sense of belonging and providing opportunities to socialize as well as to contribute something meaningful to the community. Participants also spoke in detail about the cognitive benefits that were associated with meeting new challenges, learning new skills, and staying mentally active through musical activities that required concentration and memory. Many individuals told stories of how music generated positive emotions and functioned as protection against stress and depression. Older people spoke of how music-making provided a vehicle for creative expression, enhanced confidence, and feelings of rejuvenation. Participants referred to being a 'musician' – a new or rediscovered role involving new skills, interest, and a sense of social affirmation and affiliation.

In Section 1: Music-making and wellbeing, we review the international literature concerned with the social and emotional (Chapter 2), cognitive

---

1 Throughout the book, in line with Betts Adams *et al.* (2011) we use the terms wellbeing and quality of life interchangeably.

(Chapter 3), and physical benefits (Chapter 4) of music-making amongst older people. We link key messages from this body of research with theoretical ideas about quality of life and subjective wellbeing. Our unequivocal view is that engagement with music-making has the potential to support sustained wellbeing through the latter stages of life, thus contributing to active ageing.

Section 2: Musical development and quality in facilitation, teaching, and learning, begins with an exploration of the potential for musical development, amongst older people (Chapter 5). This is an area that has been very largely ignored in the music education and psychology of music literature where, for the most part, discussion of musical development has focused on children and young adults. However, it has been claimed that all humans have a musical reserve capacity – an underused part of fundamental human musicality – that can be activated and developed at any stage in the lifecourse (Gembris, 2012). We argue that musical development is possible across the lifespan and that older people *can* and *do* progress as musicians.

The principles and practices of facilitating groups of older people, with specific reference to musical groups, are discussed in Chapter 6. Here, the focus is on interpersonal and pedagogical issues that characterize effective practice in facilitating community music activities for older people. Implications for practice are highlighted, with recommendations for how musical activities for older people may function most effectively as a creative, empathetic response to some of the challenges of ageing such as stress, isolation, and depression.

The final chapter of Section 2 focuses on intergenerational music-making (Chapter 7), demonstrating that this is a rich context for cross-generational interdependence, solidarity, and peer learning. The idea of generativity (Erikson, 1963), referring to the importance for older adults of making a lasting contribution, is applied in the discussion of how intergenerational music-making may foster wider benefits for younger people as well as supporting quality of life and subjective wellbeing during the Third and Fourth Ages. Case-study examples of the challenges and benefits of intergenerational groups are framed by background literature relating to intergenerational learning and collaboration.

Section 3: Supporting access to musical participation amongst older people, considers factors that support or constrain access to musical participation amongst older people. The contexts for musical participation that may best support the reported positive outcomes are discussed in Chapter 8. Practical and ethical issues relating to accessibility, resources, and use of space are highlighted, drawing on evidence from participants as well as from facilitators of musical activities for older people. Potential barriers to participation, including structural, intrapersonal, and social barriers are explored in Chapter 9, alongside some case-study examples of potential solutions.

Finally, the concluding Chapter 10 draws together the themes of active ageing, active participation in music, and wellbeing. Key points emerging from the background literature are summarized and contextualized within the framework of a model for wellbeing developed through the Music for Life Project. Implications and recommendations are offered, aimed at:

- older people who are interested in participating in musical activities
- care-givers who are interested in supporting older people with engagement in music
- facilitators of musical activities
- funders and policy makers with influence over 'arts for health' initiatives.

Our ageing population

A major demographic transition is underway, with the world's population aged 60 and above set to rise from 841 million in 2013 to three billion in 2100 (United Nations, 2013). Particularly steep increases in absolute numbers of older people will occur in developing countries, notably China, Brazil, and Nigeria. All over the world, the proportion of the population aged 60 and over is increasing; by the year 2050 some of the most aged countries will be Japan, Spain, Italy, Germany, and Portugal, where those aged 60+ will account for between 38 and 43 per cent of their populations (United Nations, 2013).

In the UK the number of people over 65 is projected to double by 2071, reaching 21.3 million (Government Office for Science, 2008), while in the USA the proportion of the population in this age bracket is projected to reach 13 per cent by 2030 (Coffman, 2002). The number of people aged over 80 is rising rapidly and in the UK is expected to reach 9.5 million by 2071 (Government Office for Science, 2008). Amongst our ageing population, the proportion representing the 'oldest old' (over 85) is particularly notable. The UK Office for National Statistics (2010) estimated that the number of centenarians in England and Wales had increased by 84 per cent, between 2000 and 2010. In England alone this age group is projected to rise from 10,200 in 2009 to 48,500 in 2028 (Audit Commission, 2008). Globally, it is estimated that centenarians will number one million by 2030 (Yong, 2009).

This extraordinary demographic transition may be seen, in part, as a triumph of public health policies (WHO, 2002), yet has posed many challenges. For example, significant problems relating to the prevalence of social isolation and depression amongst older people have been noted (Age

Concern, 2008; Chang-Quan *et al.*, 2010; RRA, 2010). Furthermore, the incidence of chronic disease amongst older adults is on the rise, requiring cost-effective and compassionate responses (Lafortune and Balestat, 2007; Naughton *et al.*, 2006). Within this context, there is an accepted need for initiatives that support older people's health, participation, and security (WHO, 2002).

The Third and Fourth Ages

Within the rapidly changing demographic context noted above, a definition of 'older adult' is necessary. Later life has been conceptualized as comprising a Third and a Fourth phase (Laslett, 1989). Generally, Third Age seniors are thought to be in the 'crown of life', enjoying a considerable degree of independence, autonomy, cognitive functioning, and wellbeing (Boone James and Wink, 2006; Fillit *et al.*, 2002; Scourfield, 2007). In contrast, the Fourth Age is characterized as a period of gradual disengagement and dependency, involving physical and mental decline and potential decrease in subjective wellbeing (Baltes and Smith, 2003).

The Third Age has been marked as beginning at age 65, followed by a transition to the Fourth Age at about age 85 (Tesch-Römer and Wurm, 2012). Others define the age groups differently. For example, Schuller and Watson (2009) recommend that the Third Age be conceptualized as between ages 50 and 75, with the Fourth Age (the fastest growing age group in the UK) comprising those aged over 75. Although age bands have been used to explore later life transitions, the difficulty of attaching a chronological age to these phases has been acknowledged (Laslett, 1989), with some arguing that the Third Age represents a quality of life, rather than a specific age band. One guitar player in the Music for Life Project captured this blurring of chronological age categories:

> You are extremely active between fifty and seventy these days. I mean seventy is the new sixty, if you see what I mean! So between seventy and eighty you continue to be active but you feel older as you do it. And you don't really age until after eighty-four ... I don't feel any particular age; you know, some days I feel sixteen, sometimes a hundred and sixty.
>
> Toby, aged 76, Music for Life Project

Active ageing

Active ageing is directly linked with quality of life and wellbeing during the Third and Fourth Ages (Tesch-Römer and Wurm, 2012; Walker, 2008), and has been defined as 'the process of optimizing opportunities for health, participation and security to enhance the quality of life of ageing people' (WHO, 2002: 12). The World Health Organization's framework identifies key dimensions of active ageing. These include autonomy, independence, and quality of life, incorporating physical and psychological health. Active ageing – sometimes referred to as 'optimal ageing' – is thus a multidimensional concept, involving both subjective and objective variables, encompassing physical and mental function and social engagement (Brownie and Horstmanshof, 2012; Fries, 2012; Paúl *et al.*, 2012). Subjective wellbeing, in particular, has been found to be strongly related to optimal ageing (Simone and Haas, 2013).

With roots in activity theory, active ageing focuses on continuing competence, knowledge, and participation in 'social, economic, cultural, spiritual and civic affairs' (Boudiny and Mortelmans, 2011: 8). Continued engagement in social activities that involve some physical or mental effort has been identified as an important facet of active ageing, in turn supporting a sustained high quality of life (Boudiny and Mortelmans, 2011). Many advocate for a notion of active ageing that is broad and inclusive, taking account of individual needs and differences amongst those in the Third and Fourth Ages and encompassing activities that provide a sense of empowerment for even the frailest of elders (Boudiny and Mortelmans, 2011; Tesch-Römer and Wurm, 2012; Walker, 2008).

This idea of active ageing contrasts with a deficit paradigm that characterizes old age as a period of inevitable cognitive and physical decline (Withnall *et al.*, 2004; WHO, 2012). Rather, active ageing privileges the idea of plasticity, positing that old age may involve gains as well as losses (Fries, 2012; Tesch-Römer and Wurm, 2012). In accordance with this view, researchers have noted that ageing actively involves the capacity to be adaptive with regard to goals (Heckhausen, Wrosch, and Schulz, 2010). This may be interpreted as the acceptance of lost possible selves alongside the development of well-understood new possible selves (Creech *et al.*, 2013c). New, or adapted, possible selves may be in turn underpinned by 'processes of selection (choosing goals), optimization (investing resources for achieving goals), and compensation (substitution of lost resources)' (Tesch-Römer and Wurm, 2012: 167).

Owing to its complexity, measurement of active ageing is difficult. Some researchers note that perceptions of the experience of active ageing differ markedly amongst subgroups of older people defined by, for example, age, gender, ethnicity, or socioeconomic group (Boudiny and Mortelmans, 2011). However, psychological characteristics such as happiness and optimism have been found consistently to be related to wellbeing (Kotter-Grühn and Smith,

2011) and 'highly relevant in determining the individual adaptation to the ageing process' (Paúl *et al.*, 2012: 9). Thus, interventions that support social interaction and provide joyful, creative experiences may play an important role in active ageing. Music-making is one such activity; there is a growing interest in its potential to support positive wellbeing amongst older adults (Creech *et al.*, 2013a).

The universality of music and its relationship with active ageing

Music is at the very essence of our humanity (Blacking, 1995; Wallin *et al.*, 2000). For many thousands of years music, and in particular singing, has had an important role to play in the functioning of society and has played a central role in maintaining wellbeing amongst humans of all ages, across cultures and contexts.

Although some have argued that music exists simply because of the pleasure that it affords (Pinker, 1997), others have suggested a range of practical evolutionary purposes (Huron, 2003). Music has significance because of its bonding effect, its association with cooperative, collaborative group interactions, and its communicative power that is complementary to language (Cross, 2009; Hagen and Bryant, 2003).

In the latter part of our lives, music-making offers opportunities for enhancing the quality of life, thus supporting active ageing (Tesch-Römer, 2012; WHO, 2012). Through music, individuals may access social networks and experience personal development, self-expression, and a sense of empowerment (Coffman, 2002; Cohen, 2009; Creech *et al.*, 2013a). Its importance in individual lives has been found to be consistently high across the Third and Fourth Ages, irrespective of age, geographical region, or mental competence (Cohen *et al.*, 2002).

> Music I think benefits everybody, because everybody has some sort of reaction, babies, children, so music I think benefits everybody, because of its beauty ... It is an uplifting experience. I can't imagine a life without music ... It is important to me. It fulfils a need.
>
> Margaret, aged 80, Music for Life Project

The key to music's powerful relationship with wellbeing and active ageing may lie in its holistic nature. Music can be experienced physiologically (e.g. changes in heart rate), through movement, through mood and emotion, and cognitively through knowledge and memories which may be personal, or related to the style or period of the music itself. Musical engagement thus has great potential to enhance physical, social, emotional, and cognitive wellbeing, facets of the quality of life that are strongly associated with active ageing (Smith, 2000).

There are some debates about which types of leisure activities might be classified as 'active', as opposed to 'passive'. For example, Boudiny and Mortelmans (2011) point out that reading, watching television, or listening to an opera may all be 'active', depending on the mental effort on the part of the individual. Walker (2008: 87) sets out a number of principles of active ageing, amongst which is the idea that '"activity" should consist of all meaningful pursuits that contribute to the wellbeing of the individual concerned' and should be interpreted flexibly in such a way as to be inclusive of all older people, across the Third and Fourth Ages.

The focus of this book is on research concerned with music-making – activities where individual participants engage in some form of production of music, be it choir, improvisation, instrumental group, or songwriting. However, this does not preclude the notion that individuals may derive great benefit from active listening. Indeed, an inclusive approach to active ageing requires a re-examination of traditional ideas about what 'active' means and how activities are structured (Boudiny and Mortelmans, 2011; Walker, 2008). We return to this point in Chapter 6, concerned with facilitating musical engagement amongst older people.

Quality of life

Quality of life has been conceptualized both as a predictor and as an outcome of active ageing (Tesch-Römer and Wurm, 2012). Amongst the many definitions of quality of life (Smith, 2000) two main strands have emerged, one focusing on economic conditions and resources, the other on self-perceived experiences (Daatland, 2005). Although much research with older populations has treated physical health and longevity as proxies for quality of life, several authors have argued that this approach does not reflect the current social context where older people are living longer and have healthier and more active lives (Higgs *et al.*, 2003; Hodge, 1990). Some researchers have focused on self-perceptions of wellbeing, which is generally accepted as a multi-dimensional concept that underpins quality of life (Daatland, 2005) and is often understood as being synonymous with quality of life (Betts Adams *et al.*, 2011).

The Music for Life Project (Hallam *et al.*, 2011) adopted a needs satisfaction perspective, in exploring wellbeing and quality of life amongst older adults who participated in community-based musical activities. According to this perspective, quality of life and subjective wellbeing are thought to reflect the extent to which basic human needs are perceived to be met by the individual. Some have argued that attempts to define such needs may be insensitive to differences between social groups and societies and indifferent to the dynamic nature of attitudes (Allison *et al.*, 1997; Hornquist, 1990), although basic needs such as food, shelter, and warmth (Maslow, 1954) generally are not contested. While needs such as autonomy and social participation are more abstract and difficult to measure, increasingly these have been recognized as valid and vital aspects of wellbeing (Doyal and Gough, 1991). Furthermore, positive affect and personal control beliefs have been associated with cognitive and emotional wellbeing (Lang and Heckhausen, 2001), while improved self-esteem has been found to increase resilience to health adversity amongst older people (Gallacher *et al.*, 2012).

The changing nature of ageing may require a special consideration of what might be construed as essential psychological needs in the latter part of our lives. Some have argued that as increasing numbers of people remain active, relatively healthy, and keen to develop a variety of leisure interests (Scase and Scales, 2000), the psychological needs for social participation, autonomy and choice are particularly salient.

McKenna *et al.* (1999) suggest that models relating to older adult life need to move away from a focus on function and emphasize the reasons why individuals want to accomplish things. From this perspective, leisure activities and social networking provide the means by which needs may be fulfilled. In this way, lifestyle, comprising goal directed activities and social relationships, may be seen as the narrative of self (Higgs *et al.*, 2003). Self-narrative (the stories that people use to construct meaning out of the events of their lives), underpinned by agency and autonomy, in turn becomes the route to self-actualization. Daatland (2005: 375–6) supports this view, suggesting that 'successful ageing, and indeed quality of life, has to do with the road (process) more than the destination (end state) – to have goals and a motivation to try and reach them'.

While basic needs are thought to remain stable over the lifecourse, their relative salience changes over time. Steverink and Lindberg (2006) proposed a model of basic needs that comprises affection, behavioural confirmation, and status. Affection is fulfilled when individuals feel liked, loved, trusted, accepted, and empathized with in relationships. Behavioural confirmation refers to the feeling of doing things well, contributing to a common goal, and playing a useful part in a functional group, while status is fulfilled when individuals are treated with respect, have skills or qualities that are recognized and when they are independent and autonomous. The model was tested in the Netherlands with a sample of 1322 community-dwelling people aged 65–98 (mean age 74), treating measures of these three needs as potential predictors of reported wellbeing. The results indicated that, as expected, older people experienced loss in terms of satisfaction of their needs for behavioural confirmation and status. However, the importance of these needs did not diminish with advancing age or with increasing levels of physical decline, even when older people experienced high levels of affection.

Higgs *et al.* (2003) drew attention to the positive dimensions of ageing. Their model of essential needs stresses the role of control and autonomy in sustaining full personal and social development through later years and includes self-realization as well as the pursuit of pleasurable activities. These dimensions of control and autonomy, they argue, underpin self-realization and pleasure. Autonomy and control may thus be conceptualized as internal resources to be exploited in pursuit of activities that foster pleasure, fulfil goals, and provide a sense of purpose.

Self-determination theory is also relevant to research on the ageing population (Deci and Ryan, 2000). Here basic needs are conceptualized as competence, autonomy, and relatedness. These must be satisfied in a sustained fashion in order for humans to function optimally as they strive for effectiveness, connectedness, and coherence. From this perspective, the presence or absence of environmental conditions that facilitate the satisfaction of these needs may be a predictor of mental health and vitality. These environmental conditions might include factors such as social belonging or having interesting, revitalizing, and challenging goals.

Measuring basic needs satisfaction in a musical context

The Music for Life Project, offered in this book as a case-study example of active ageing through music, examined the extent to which basic psychological needs could be satisfied by the process of engaging with music-making in community settings. The quantitative measures adopted to assess wellbeing were the CASP-12 measure of quality of life (Higgs *et al.*, 2003) and the Basic Psychological Needs test (Deci and Ryan, 2000). Specific findings relating to these scales are reported in Section 1 of this book.

The CASP-12 measure of quality of life amongst older people uses a four-point Likert scale to measure the underlying dimensions of control and autonomy, self-realization, and pleasure. Control is conceptualized as the ability to actively intervene in one's environment, while autonomy is the right to be free from the unwanted interference of others. Self-realization represents 'the more reflexive nature of life', while pleasure refers to 'the sense of fun derived from the more active (doing) aspects of life' (Wiggins *et al.*, 2007: 5).

Initially, 19 Likert scale items were piloted with a postal survey of 264 people aged 65–75 across England and Scotland. The sample was drawn from participants who had been followed up from the Boyd-Orr survey of childhood diet and health in the 1930s (Hyde *et al.*, 2003). Following this, confirmatory analyses were carried out with samples drawn from the first wave of the English Longitudinal Study of Ageing (ELSA_1; N = 9300) and the 11th wave of the British Household Panel Survey (BHPS_11; N = 6471). Both of these nationally representative surveys were conducted in 2002 and consisted of respondents aged 55 and above. Internal consistency for the ELSA study, calculated using Cronbach Alpha scores, for the self-realization (0.77), pleasure (0.8) and control (0.67) sub-scales were moderate to high, but lower for autonomy (0.45). For the BHPS study the scores were: control (0.66), autonomy (0.46), self-realization (0.76) and pleasure (0.77). Following further analyses, the researchers reduced the overall number of items to 12 and combined the control and autonomy sub-scales, raising Cronbach's Alpha for the new sub-scale to 0.67. The shortened 12-item version of CASP was found to have stronger measurement properties than the original CASP-19 measure and was recommended for future applications (Wiggins *et al.*, 2007).

The second measure of wellbeing adopted in the Music for Life Project was the Basic Psychological Needs Scales (Deci and Ryan, 2000). This scale has 21 items assessed on a seven-point scale. The three subscales are conceptualized as competence, autonomy, and relatedness. An extensive body of research demonstrates a relationship between wellbeing and satisfaction of these three subscales (see Johnston and Finney, 2010, for a review). Gagné (2003) reported Cronbach Alpha values for the three sub-scales as: autonomy = 0.69; relatedness = 0.86; and competence = 0.71. The overall 21-item index of general need satisfaction produced a Cronbach Alpha value of 0.89. Although the scale has been used extensively, there has been little in the way of rigorous study of its psychometric properties (Johnston and Finney, 2010) but as the conceptual framework is similar to the CASP-12 it was considered appropriate to provide triangulation.

Active ageing through music: a revised model of wellbeing (basic needs satisfaction)

The Music for Life Project team explored whether the CASP-12 and Basic Psychological Needs scales together might reveal an underlying model that could help to explain how wellbeing and active ageing was supported amongst older people, through participation in community musical activities. To this end, a principal component analysis was undertaken to explore the relationships between the two measures of quality of life (CASP-12 and Basic Psychological Needs Scale) (for details of the analysis see Creech *et al.*, 2013b; Hallam *et al.*, 2013). This analysis revealed three underlying factors. Factor 1 related to a sense of purpose and a positive outlook on life. Factor 2 was concerned with self-perceptions of autonomy and control, while Factor 3 focused on positive social relationships, competence and a sense of recognized accomplishment (Figure 1.1).

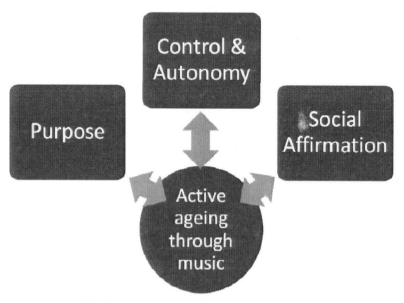

Figure 1.1: Model of basic needs satisfaction through music

Factor 1 (purpose) had high weightings related to enjoyment, looking forward to each day, feeling that life had meaning and was full of opportunities, that the future looked good, that participants were full of energy and could do what they wanted (see Table 1.1). Factor 2 (autonomy and control, or lack thereof) related to the extent to which individuals felt in control, competent, and capable. This factor, which was largely comprised of items that were framed negatively, also reflected the extent to which participants perceived themselves to be pressured, left out of things, and with few opportunities to undertake activities. Factor 3 (social affirmation) had high weightings related to social factors such as getting along with people, liking people, having friends, and being cared about. It also included elements relating to recognition for being good at things, being accomplished, and being able to express ideas and learn new things.

The revised model reflects alternative conceptions of self-perceived wellbeing in older people. The first factor, sense of purpose in life (enjoyment, having opportunities, feeling positive, and looking forward to each day), has clear links with the CASP-12 measures of pleasure and self-realization (Wiggins *et al.*, 2007). The second factor, concerned with autonomy and control, appears in many frameworks for quality of life and wellbeing (Deci and Ryan, 2000; Higgs *et al.*, 2003; Baltes and Smith, 2003; Steverink and Lindenberg, 2006; Wiggins *et al.*, 2007). The third factor, social affirmation, includes elements of Deci and Ryan's concept of relatedness but has stronger links with Steverink and Lindenberg's model that sets out needs for affection, behavioural confirmation, and status.

Table 1.1: The three factors and their weightings

	Factor		
	1	2*	3
	Purpose	Autonomy/ control	Social affirmation
I enjoy the things that I do	.819		
I look forward to each day	.812		
I feel that my life has meaning	.785		
I feel that the future looks good for me	.760	−.269	
I feel that life is full of opportunities	.738	−.264	
I feel full of energy these days	.678	−.347	
I can do the things I want to do	.633		
I feel that I can please myself in what I do	.560		
I feel that what happens to me is out of my control		.631	
Often, I do not feel very competent		.585	
I often do not feel very capable		.576	
I feel pressured in my life		.557	
I feel left out of things		.539	−.271
There is not much opportunity for me to decide for myself how to do things in my daily life	−.219	.537	
My age prevents me from doing the things I would like to do	−.286	.518	
In my life I do not get much of a chance to show how capable I am		.479	
In my daily life, I frequently have to do what I'm told		.417	
I pretty much keep to myself and don't have a lot of social contacts		.410	−.272

There are not many people that I am close to		.407	−.254
Shortage of money stops me from doing things I want to do		.356	
The people I interact with regularly do not seem to like me much		.316	
I get along with people I come into contact with			.730
I really like the people I interact with			.662
I consider the people I regularly interact with to be my friends			.646
People are generally pretty friendly towards me			.592
People in my life care about me		−.207	.581
People I know tell me I am good at what I do			.518
Most days I feel a sense of accomplishment from what I do	.343	−.335	.500
I generally feel free to express my ideas and opinions		−.332	.490
I have been able to learn interesting new skills recently	.234		.464
I feel like I can pretty much be myself in my daily situations		−.307	.412
I feel like I am free to decide for myself how to live my life		−.323	.407
People I interact with on a daily basis tend to take my feelings into consideration			.294

*These items are framed negatively, meaning that negative factor loadings indicate higher perceptions of autonomy and control, while positive factor loadings indicate lower perceptions of autonomy and control.

Application of the revised model of wellbeing

Throughout this book, personal stories drawn from interviews and focus groups with Music for Life Project participants will demonstrate how the revised model can help to explain how active music-making in a social context has the potential to enhance the quality of life, and physical and mental health in older people. In addition, examples from the wider research concerned with music-making amongst older people will be drawn together, making a case for high quality musical participation as a vehicle for active ageing.

Section One

Music-making and wellbeing

1

Chapter 2

Musical social networks and social-emotional wellbeing

This chapter focuses on the reported social and emotional benefits of participation in musical activities. We foreground the Music for Life Project; individual stories provide insight with regard to how participation in musical groups offered pathways to positive social and emotional wellbeing. Individual examples are framed by background literature that links musical social networks, active ageing, and subjective social and emotional wellbeing.

Social networks

Face-to-face social networks have been found to play a critical role in sustaining quality of life amongst older people (Brownie and Horstmanshof, 2012; Heenan, 2011). Characterized by the availability of interpersonal relationships and the potential for practical and emotional support, social networks provide 'ties to society through participation ... and social roles' (Thomése *et al.*, 2005: 463). Social networks support personal engagement in both optional (discretionary, done by choice) and obligatory (necessary to everyday life) domains (Schindler *et al.*, 2006). There is strong evidence that participation in social networks may have positive implications for physiological and psychological health (e.g. Cohen and Doyle, 1997; Smith and Christakis, 2008), decrease the risk of dementia (Cacioppo *et al.*, 2000), and increase happiness amongst the individual members (Fowler and Christakis, 2008; Litwin and Shiovitz-Ezra, 2011).

> The camaraderie, the social activity is almost important as whatever it is you're doing. I'm going to be 73 this year, so it's easy at our age, especially, you know I'm arthritic, I've got some limitations in my mobility, it would be easy for me to vegetate, particularly over winter, but getting up and going to the classes, you get up, you get yourself showered and dressed and everything and off you go. That part of it is as important as what you're learning.
>
> Glenn, aged 72, Music for Life Project

In the latter phases of life when loss of close relationships is often experienced, friendship and support from a social network 'contributes to the maintenance of a sense that life is meaningful' (Setterson, 2002: 67). Social networks help older people to maintain meaningful social roles, remaining integrated with others who share similar values, as well as establishing new contacts and accessing new ideas and resources (George, 2005).

Since the 1980s, when a link between social networks and health outcomes was recognized, researchers have been interested in understanding the specific facets of social support, personal relationships, and networks that are beneficial for ageing.

Gerontological network researchers have identified several social network characteristics (Thomése *et al.*, 2005). Social networks may be based on attachment, roles, and exchange of support. The network structure reflects changes that occur as individuals age, with lost role relationships accompanied by increased importance placed on close family and friendships. The idea of 'social exchange' refers to the need for reciprocity and balanced exchange within a network, with a strong correlation between giving and receiving support. From this view, over-benefited individuals may feel overly dependent, supporting the view that social networks may most effectively support wellbeing when individuals continue to feel that they can give and receive, be it instrumental or emotional support. Finally, networks are also underpinned by 'individual choice'; older people invest in social networks selectively, in order to achieve emotionally meaningful goals.

Social networks as a context for active ageing

Social networks with meaningful leisure activities as their focus have been described as 'proximate social contexts' that bring meaning and a sense of purpose to life (Setterson, 2002). Socially oriented leisure activities, as compared with solitary activities, may be particularly favourable with regard to positive quality of life (Simone and Haas, 2013). Across several countries and cultures, older people who participate in social activities have been found to benefit from access to socio-emotional support and a reduced risk of social isolation and loneliness (Betts Adams *et al.*, 2011). In particular, social intimacy and warmth that is fostered by certain collaborative activities 'appears to be a very important, if not the most important, aspect of engagement that influences wellbeing' (Betts Adams *et al.*, 2011: 705).

Relative freedom from obligation during old age may be interpreted as an opportunity, providing a context for engagement in creative and meaningful activity, developing new goals, and exploring new possible selves. However, it may also pose the great risk of a loss of sense of purpose. 'Without obligation life can become empty of meaning: boredom or depression may appear as an accompaniment to loss of purpose or usefulness' (Setterson, 2002: 70–1). Thus, social leisure activities have the potential to function as much more than a way to fill time and keep busy, offering a context where new role relationships may develop, a sense of belonging may flourish, and a sense of purpose may be sustained.

Just as at any other phase of life, older adults deserve a life that is 'rich in experience and engagement' (Setterson, 2002: 71). Positive wellbeing has been linked with social leisure activities amongst those in the Third Age as well as elder adults with varying functional capacity, including those living in residential care or assisted living. The need for creative approaches to maintaining social networks associated with leisure activities for adults in the Fourth Age, or indeed for any older adults who face psychological, physiological, or structural barriers to participation, is particularly salient. Research has shown that the more frail individuals perceive themselves to be, the less likely they will engage in leisure activity. Reduced participation, in turn, is associated with a lower sense of social belonging, having a detrimental impact on subjective wellbeing (Simone and Haas, 2013). Rather than being a certain predictor of disengagement, declining health or vitality may be mitigated with compassionate and creative approaches to the structure and facilitation of social networks. In this vein, meaningful social activities require a responsive approach to the needs and aspirations of the older people themselves, including consultation with constituents with regard to the group structure and the nature and extent of mental and physical demands (Betts Adams *et al.*, 2011; Heenan, 2011).

Musical social networks: social wellbeing

Music-making involves a strong 'element of sociability' (Finnegan, 1989: 328). Previous research concerned with music and ageing has attributed significant social benefits amongst senior citizens to their involvement in community-based musical social networks (see Coffman, 2002; Creech *et al.*, 2013a; Lehmberg and Fung, 2010). Social networks that are centred around group singing, songwriting, and a range of instrumental music-making involving diverse musical genres, have been found to support group identity, collaborative learning, friendship, social support, and a strong feeling of belonging amongst group members.

Amongst the participants in the Music for Life Project, there was strong agreement with the view that music helped them to remain involved with their communities. Indeed, music facilitators in the Music for Life Project observed that their groups sometimes had profound positive social consequences. Facilitators noted that through collaborative music-making, participants developed a deep sense of being connected with other group members (Box 2.1)

Box 2.1 Musical social networks – a facilitator's perspective

I think that for a lot of people, where there is something that they thought 'we'll try', I think that now it's part of their life. And that's why they don't like the long, big holidays because it's something that they do so regularly and it's … They meet their friends, they come here, it's a real routine for them. And I think for some people, it's totally transformed their life because it has given them another whole world to belong to.

We can't imagine, I don't think, the loneliness that some people suffer. You know, we laugh that if we have a ten o'clock session [the participants] will be here at half past eight; if we have a five o'clock session they'll be here at lunch time because that is the day. … A lady used to come in every Tuesday but she used to come at least an hour early and sit there … At the end of term she put a bottle of wine on my desk and a card that said 'I just want to thank you for giving me a life after my husband died'.

That's the beauty of music, it really pulls people together, and once you've played music with somebody, especially if you've gone out and performed it, you're always going to be more connected than you ever were before.

Facilitator, Music for Life Project, community choir and instrumental groups

---

The Music for Life Project reinforced the findings from earlier research concerned with music as a social resource, amongst older people. Langston and Barrett (2008) provide an example of social connection in a community choir in regional Tasmania, where 27 choir members (the majority of whom were retired) were interviewed. The choir was found to be a strong community resource, fostering trust, learning, interaction, participation, and civic involvement. The choir members were united by a strong sense of fellowship that was generated through singing together. This sense of fellowship, attributed with equal importance to the music itself, was derived from 'trust, camaraderie, togetherness, friendship, warmth, support, and deep appreciation of the feelings and needs of members' (Langston, 2011: 178).

Similarly, Wood's (2010: 167) ethnographic study of the 'Singing Diplomats' – a choir comprising 22 senior (aged approximately 68 years) Russian immigrants in Jerusalem – portrayed this musical social network as an empowering and 'rich expressive space'. Singing together became a shared musical, social, and emotional experience through which choir members developed their identity as a group.

Robust social relationships were likewise found amongst participants in the 'Happy Wanderers', a small choir comprising ten Third Age seniors, whose purpose was to perform for residents of care homes and older people with dementia (Southcott, 2009). The choir had been in existence for 14 years, had a repertoire of over 600 songs by memory, and voluntarily undertook in excess of a hundred concerts per year. Choir members described themselves as a 'friendship group who support each other as a family would' (Southcott, 2009: 148). Some of the original members had made a transition into residential care, but still maintained strong social bonds with the group, continuing to sing together when possible. Reporting on the work of the Happy Wanderers, Motte (2004) quotes one choir member who elaborated this theme, stating that:

> It's always good to get together … Such a strong bond between us. Each of us has been through tough times – marriage breakup, loss of spouse or child, wayward offspring, serious health problems, a mental breakdown or loneliness. For over 11 years the group has been a haven where members find acceptance, understanding, comfort and a place to regain strength.
>
> (Motte 2004: 28, cited in Southcott, 2009: 150)

Like the 'Happy Wanderers', participants in the Music for Life Project described how music was a vehicle for bringing people together in a meaningful activity. Tremendous importance was attached to being able to share their music-making within the community, particularly making links with Fourth Age people who were in residential care or hospitals. For Jack (Box 2.2), music provided continuity in his life. His choir also provided a sense of social affirmation through opportunities to perform and make a positive difference in the lives of others.

> ## Box 2.2 A highly valued musical social network
>
> Jack (aged 85) has always loved singing. As a boy he participated in the synagogue choir, where he received much positive and warm feedback for his singing. He loves all types of music, especially musicals and 'old songs'. He has dedicated 63 years of service to a charity for disabled war veterans, where he has made a particularly distinguished contribution as Entertainments Officer.
>
> > I feel that the group that I'm in is – people more or less my age, we're old age pensioners – ... I think it's the music. It seems that people I've never met in my life, we're closer, we're much closer together now than when I first them ... and it seems that when we're up there as a group, it's got some meaning to it. It means a lot to us, it means a lot to our group leader, and when we go out from here sometimes to hospitals or other old people's homes and we sing to them, it's marvellous ... I wouldn't care if I was asked to go out three or four times a week to sing to other people because I get – I'm afraid I'm a bit of an emotional one [tearful] but I get a wonderful feeling inside me to see the happiness it gives to these other people because – one day actually I went to the hospital because I had a relation of mine, an old aunt who was in that hospital, and I sung her a couple of songs in the ward and all these old ladies knew the tunes, and I finished up doing the same thing twice and the second time they all joined in. We did one [a concert] to one of the old people's homes and a lady who used to be in our choir is now there as a resident and she, that day we had her sitting with us back in the choir which was lovely for her ... It gives me, at my age [tearful] I'm 85, it gives me a great feeling inside me that I can sing and it makes other people happy.
> >
> > Jack, aged 85, Music for Life Project

Music has been shown to be a powerful tool in constructing a sense of community within a residential care context. Allison (2008) carried out an ethnographic study focusing on a songwriting group of approximately 30 members with an average age of 87, who met every four to six weeks for intensive facilitated songwriting sessions. The group was diverse with regard to physical and cognitive functional limitations. While some members were entirely independent, others had significant physical dependence and dementia. The group was facilitated in working collaboratively towards their goal of writing a 'good' song. Facilitators respected the collective group wisdom and the knowledge and insight of the participants. In drawing upon their life experiences, participants demonstrated great diversity, yet also, through the collaborative process, constructed a common heritage. As the sessions progressed participants became increasingly engaged and animated. The songwriting group offered an enabling environment in which participants responded to creative and intellectual challenges in ways that were vibrant, creative, and productive. Through songwriting the older people continued to learn new skills, producing tangible cultural outputs that became an enduring part of the culture of the residential community.

Engagement with making music in instrumental groups has, like singing and songwriting, been found to be associated with role replacement, social cohesion, and belongingness. Several researchers have reported the social benefits experienced by members of wind bands such as those in the New Horizons Band network in the USA. For example, Ernst and Emmons (1992) reported that in some senses the band could function as a replacement for the workplace; band members typically developed new friendships and a strong attachment to the group. Alongside the shared music-making, social ties were strengthened in practical ways such as scheduling social time around the rehearsals and outreach activities (Dabback, 2008a). Similarly, Coffman and Adamek (2001) reported that 33 older people, participating together in a volunteer concert band, described a strong sense of bonding and support, while Dabback (2008a) described a sense of belonging and collaboration amongst band members.

The Music for Life Project reinforced these earlier reports relating to older people's engagement in musical social networks (Hallam *et al.*, 2012; Varvarigou *et al.*, 2012a). Participants in a wide range of musical groups noted consistently that music activities gave a purpose and structure to their life after retirement, providing an activity to look forward to every week. Participants were motivated to make the effort to attend the groups, which were described as fun and enjoyable places where participants felt a sense of community as well as personal fulfilment. Through participation in musical groups, individuals were able to socialize with like-minded people, to work together as a team, and to belong to a group that supported their musical aspirations (Box 2.3).

Box 2.3 Musical social networks – purpose and structure to their life after retirement

For forty years, Albert (aged 80) and Stella (aged 79) had been involved in local operatic society productions. Following retirement, and because of the 'demise' of operatic societies owing to lack of younger members joining, they joined a choir, looking for a 'different outlet'.

> People – after they have finished their professional careers – the horizons obviously narrow. Coming to a place like this they start expanding again ... Once you retire from professional life, your working life and so on and so forth, obviously your circle becomes so much smaller. Your environment is so much smaller. You haven't got the social interaction ... whereas coming to a group like this where you can interact once again ... But certainly the singing element, the fact that you have to stand up there and sing ... I always find, when I sing that it gives me a lift ... the bonhomie of it all, you know. You are happy, you are having a joke with your neighbour. Yes ... It's certainly the interaction between people, which is very, very important ... There is no question about that.
>
> Albert, aged 80, and Stella, aged 79, Music for Life Project

---

Like Albert and Stella (Box 2.3), Nima described forming new social networks through music. For Nima, music-making brought her into contact with new ideas amongst people with whom she would not otherwise have found a bond (Box 2.4).

Box 2.4 New routine – new friends – a fresh outlook

Nima lives alone, and was encouraged by a friend to join a choir after she retired and was looking for a new routine in her life. She loves music but has never participated in a group before, despite the fact that she has been surrounded by music in her family. Both of her parents played the piano by ear, her brother is a keen jazz fan, and her daughter played the recorder in school. During her working life she occasionally went to the opera, and often listened to her collection of records, with favourites being 'light classics'.

Most of the people in that group are people that I probably wouldn't have socialized with in any way, are really extremely knowledgeable, they know about operas, they know everything about everything and it's been interesting ... and there are people there who are talented ... I've never been part of a [music]group, this is the first, and I've learned a lot I have to say, I've learned a tremendous amount ... I just find the people very, very interesting ... people I would have passed in the street, this sounds snobby but it isn't because we all have different interests and probably educated differently, but I probably would have passed in the street without even thinking, they're so interesting, and their knowledge of composers, it's really fascinating ... It's entirely different to anything I have ever done, so here I am chatting about something which I would never have known so I think it's a tremendous benefit ... it brings people together so I think a musical activity is a wonderful thing.

Nima, aged 67, Music for Life Project participant

Music-making and psychological wellbeing

The previous section shows how musical social networks can represent a pathway to enhanced subjective wellbeing, offering social support, belongingness, and access to new social roles and relationships. Throughout the latter stages of the lifecourse, and regardless of cognitive capacity (Cohen *et al.*, 2002) or musical background (Hays and Minichiello, 2005), music-making has the potential to contribute to psychological wellbeing in a number of other ways, beyond the social benefits. Participation in music has been described by older people as 'a way to survive', 'reviving' and 'a breathing hole in my life' (Forssen, 2007: 231). Adults in the Third and Fourth Ages have spoken of a sense of 'inner happiness, inner contentment, inner satisfaction, and inner peace' (Hays and Minichiello, 2005: 269), linking these positive feelings to making music together. Listening to music and playing musical instruments have been described by community-dwelling elders as 'restorative activities' – activities that 'enable a person to feel refreshed, rested, at peace, clear-headed, and mentally able to take on new tasks and challenges' (Jansen, 2005: 37).

An early experimental study that investigated the relationship between emotional wellbeing and music-making was carried out by VanderArk *et al.* (1983). Twenty nursing home residents aged 60–95 were assigned to an experimental group that took part in twice-weekly music sessions for five weeks. During these sessions the group sang familiar songs and used simple percussion for accompaniment. A further 23 seniors, matched for age, were assigned to a comparison group where there was no music-making. In comparison with their peers, the music-makers experienced considerable benefits, with significant improvements in positive life satisfaction and musical self-concept.

Since the 1980s many more studies have illustrated the relationship between music-making and subjective wellbeing (Lehmberg and Fung, 2010). For example, a review of eight pieces of research concerned with the benefits of group singing amongst adults aged over 50 revealed that singing together was linked with wellbeing in a number of ways (Clift *et al.*, 2010). In addition to encouraging social participation, group singing was found to reduce anxiety and depression (Wise *et al.*, 1992; Houston *et al.*, 1998; Zanini and Leao, 2006; Lally, 2009; Sandgren, 2009).

The notion of a 'therapeutic choir' for the Third Age was proposed by Zanini and Leao (2006) as an intervention which would protect against decline in subjective wellbeing. Their study of 26 members of a Brazilian community choir (average age 69) revealed that singing was experienced as a means for self-expression and self-fulfilment, and that participation in the choir fostered positive feelings about the future. Similar findings were reported by Lally (2009), with regard to the Australian 'Sweet Tonic' choir, which involved 26 older people aged 51–83. Following participation in the series of 30 workshops and associated concerts the Sweet Tonic singers reported improvements in happiness and good spirits, self-confidence, and general relaxation.

The therapeutic nature of choral singing was also demonstrated by Cohen *et al.* (2006), in the USA. After one year of participation, senior chorale members (average age 80 years) reported enhanced positive self-assessments of overall health and demonstrated sustained active, independent living. Likewise in Scotland, long-term improvements to the quality of life were attributed to participation in community singing. The majority of 75 choir members, who had participated in the choir for between 7 and 11 years since reaching the statutory retirement age, described noticeable positive changes in emotional wellbeing, self-confidence, and social life, attributing these changes to their singing activities (Hillman, 2002).

A recent study in the UK has added strong support for the idea that singing in groups is a cost effective way to support positive mental health (Clift *et al.*, 2012). The study recruited 265 older volunteer participants (average age 67) who were randomly allocated to either take part in a weekly Silver Song Club for 12 weeks (the intervention group), or to take part in the comparison group, who carried on with their lives and did not participate in a singing group. All of the participants completed measures of mental health, before the Silver Song Clubs started, immediately following the 12 weeks of participation, and again three months after the Silver Song Clubs had finished. Amongst those who participated in the Silver Song Clubs, significantly greater improvements in mental health were found, as compared with those who did not participate. This effect was greatest immediately after the 12 weeks of participation, but was still evident three months later. Morrison and Clift (2012b) explain these therapeutic outcomes, noting that singing together can be a joyful activity that fosters positive feelings and raises expectations for the quality of life. In addition, participants benefit from enhanced self-belief, learning new skills, and acquiring social support networks.

Likewise, making music together in instrumental groups has been found to contribute to positive mental health, offering opportunities for alleviating loneliness and coping with various challenges of ageing. Elderly wind band members, for example, have described their music-making as an 'essential' aspect of their quality of life, rating it in importance alongside relationships with family members and health (Coffman and Adamek, 2001). For these seniors, their band functioned as a personally enriching social space. Similarly, 308 survey responses from community orchestra members from Germany, Austria, and Switzerland (aged 40–97; average age 71 years) demonstrated that these orchestras were perceived as important sources of increased vitality, quality of life, and happiness (Gembris, 2008).

There is extensive evidence of the impact of music on moods and emotions. Music, itself, can generate feelings of wellbeing, can facilitate working through difficult emotions, and is frequently linked to spirituality (Juslin and Sloboda, 2010). In accordance with the research that has linked music with emotional states, music has been found to contribute to psychological wellbeing amongst older people, through its capacity to act as a powerful medium for emotional self-regulation. For example, a qualitative study of 21 Finnish adults aged 21–70 (ten were aged 65+) suggested that seniors aged 65+, just like their younger adult counterparts, used music for 'happy mood maintenance, revival, strong sensation, diversion, discharge, mental work, solace, and psyching up' (Saarikallio, 2011: 6).

Emotional wellbeing was a prominent theme in the Music for Life Project. A wealth of qualitative data linked music participation with positive emotional states and suggested that music-making boosted resilience in the face of challenging life events. For example, individuals in the Music for Life Project described how participation in music had helped them to cope effectively with stress, depression, and bereavement. The participants attributed many positive feelings to singing and playing musical instruments – these included a sense of rejuvenation, an emotional 'lift', and spirituality. Participation in music offered opportunities for creative expression and in many cases provided a sense of purpose in life. One choir member used the word 'euphoria' to describe her feelings as she departed from choir rehearsal.

Participants in the Music for Life Project described music-making as an important emotional resource. Rosa (Box 2.5) and Leroy (Box 2.6) illustrate how music influences their mood, helped them to concentrate, and contributed to feeling calm and centred.

BOX 2.5 MUSIC AS A CREATIVE VEHICLE FOR EMOTIONAL SELF-REGULATION

Rosa (aged 76) comes from a family where there was 'no music'. She remembers 'messing about' in a school choir. Later, as a young adult, she developed an interest in 'classic' music that she heard on the radio. She now sings in a large hundred-voice choir as well as a small singing and percussion group. Her musical taste is eclectic, but she particularly loves 'songs that you can recognize, that tell a story'.

> I think as far as I'm concerned, the benefit of music is for everyone. If you're stressful ... it calms you down, it gives you a centre point ... other people have a way of relaxing by exercise or doing manic running around, but I think music is the best, apart from painting. Those two things because they're artistic, painting and singing are the most wonderful things to get into people's soul, shall we say, or heart ... that's what I'm saying about, music is very important. I can't think of a world without music.
>
> Rosa, aged 76, Music for Life Project

The pleasure of taking part in musical activities and the resulting positive effect on wellbeing was reiterated by facilitators of the Music for Life Project groups. Enhanced self-confidence, a benefit of musical participation that elsewhere has been linked with psychological wellbeing (Lally, 2009;

Lehmberg and Fung, 2010), was noted by facilitators in the Music for Life Project. This was very marked in some cases, supported by observations of participants seeming to be empowered, active, and 'adventurous' in participation (Box 2.7).

BOX 2.6 MUSIC HELPS TO BE COOL AND COLLECTED

Leroy comes from Trinidad, where he learnt Calypso from an early age, from his grandfather. For the past 15 years he has been a member of a band, playing maracas and singing. The band does regular gigs, including many for residential care homes and hospitals. Recently he has joined a choir, for the first time. Music is a central part of his life.

> The choir singing, I never done choir singing, I sing in church but I never sing in a choir, so it's something new to me ... I look forward to every Tuesday to meet, there are 16 of us, the same faces, and singing together, I look forward to that, and there's very nice people the crowd we've got, and it's the discipline, it disciplines everybody, that's what I like about it. It help you to, if you got a bad temper, it help you to be cool and collective [sic], and you can talk to somebody, even when you leave the music, you can sit down and talk to anybody, and even somebody off the handle you can sit down and say no, this is not the way, calm them. That's what I like. Understand people, why they've gone off the handle, the reason. You can do it while you're singing, the communication. Before we sing we do exercise and different things, and then the communication with each other ... so we're like a family.
>
> Leroy, aged 73, Music for Life Project participant

In some cases facilitators were aware that participants in the musical activities had ceased to take medication for depression and this was attributed to the musical engagement. Musical groups were also recognized as a context for respite for care-givers. As such, musical group activities were a way of caring for the care-givers. Facilitators evidently perceived part of their role as being to provide stress-free opportunities that supported positive mental health (Box 2.8).

Box 2.7 Increased confidence – the facilitator's perspective

There is another lady ... she was really shy and nervous and she was hanging around this room when the [choir] was going on and [one of the facilitators] saw her and she came out in the interval and said 'Do you want to come in?' She was very timid and wouldn't talk to anyone but kind of like stuck in the corner and listened for a bit and now she is one of the most confident of our participants and she is really active in the community [here] ... Considering the first one or two sessions she was so quiet, she barely spoke. I wasn't really sure if she could speak properly and she has really blossomed ... At the beginning she didn't want to do anything. She kind of said 'No, no. I just want to sit here' ... And actually she was probably the most constant person for the whole project. She is there every week and she's got slightly more adventurous.

Facilitator, Music for Life Project, Creative music

Box 2.8 Music and mental health – a facilitator's perspective

In terms of mental health, endless people have said how much this has made a difference to their lives; people who have lost partners, people who are in difficult family circumstances. ... And then people who sometimes take medication for depression or those kinds of things. When the sessions are running, they don't need to take them anymore. But when sessions stop for the summer, for example, they have to go back onto medication ... There is this magical thing about music that makes you feel good. I think that for a lot of people it really lifts the mood and you'll find for quite a lot of people who are widowed, it just provides a sort of outlet for them ... I think, it does help wellbeing, we-all-feel-it sort of thing. I think, you know, just having a chance to interact with people and

> have a good laugh. As they keep saying ...'Oh, it's a good laugh, isn't it?'
>
> A lot of our participants are carers of either their partners or their parents, who are suffering from dementia or whatever, so they have a really stressful time. And what we are doing here is providing them with that small escape where they don't have to think about any of that. I do think that's a fundamental part of what we do.
>
> Facilitator, Music for Life Project, Choral and
> instrumental groups

Quality of life: Does participation in musical social networks make a difference?

The researchers in the Music for Life Project used quantitative measures of quality of life to assess whether participation in music, as compared with other leisure activities, had a strong relationship with social and emotional wellbeing (see the Preface of this book for an account of the methodology; Chapter 1 of this book for a detailed account of the measures used). Scores for each individual on three dimensions of wellbeing (purpose, control/autonomy, and social affirmation) were used to compare those participating in the music and non-music groups. There were statistically significant differences between the groups on each factor (Table 2.1); those actively engaged with making music exhibited higher levels of subjective wellbeing, as compared with those engaged in other group activities (Creech *et al.*, 2013b).

Table 2.1: Comparison of factor scores between music and non-music groups

	Music (280)	Non-music (62)	Statistical significance
Factor 1: Sense of purpose	0.088	−0.398	0.0001*
Factor 2: Autonomy/control**	−0.068	0.310	0.007*
Factor 3: Social affirmation	0.052	−0.234	0.041*

*Values less than 0.05 indicate statistical significance.
**Negative scores on this factor indicate a positive sense of autonomy and control, as the indicators were framed negatively.

Comparisons were also made between music participants in the Third Age (up to age 75) and Fourth Age (aged 76 and over) (the same comparisons were not made for the non-music groups, owing to a small sample size of those in the Fourth Age). There were no statistically significant differences between Third and Fourth Agers on factors 2 (control/autonomy) and 3 (social affirmation). The scores on Factor 1 (sense of purpose) were lower for those in the Fourth Age (see Table 2.2). This could be interpreted as a positive finding, indicating that quality of life amongst adults participating in musical social networks was sustained through the transition to the Fourth Age, with regard to two out of the three dimensions of wellbeing.

Table 2.2: Differences in factor scores for Third and Fourth Age participants in the music groups

	Third Age (209)	Fourth Age (64)	Statistical significance
Factor 1: Purpose	0.157	–0.179	0.017*
Factor 2: Autonomy/control	–0.107	0.032	NS**
Factor 3: Social affirmation	0.060	0.056	NS**

*Values less than 0.05 indicate statistical significance.
**Not statistically significant.

These Music for Life Project findings support the results reported by Jenkins (2011), who examined changes in subjective wellbeing over a five-year period amongst a large sample (approximately 6000) drawn from the English Longitudinal Study of Ageing. Controlling for a host of demographic variables including age, gender, highest educational qualification, work status, and household income, Jenkins reported that music, arts, and evening classes were associated with significant positive changes in three measures of subjective wellbeing, while exercise classes and formal courses were not.

However, the findings reported above, that compare engagement with musical social networks with other kinds of social leisure activities, do not suggest that other leisure group activities were not valued and worthwhile. Indeed, amongst the comparison groups, responses to questions about the perceived social and emotional benefits of participation showed generally very positive responses, with little difference between the music participants and those in other groups (Hallam *et al.*, 2012) (Table 2.3).

Table 2.3: Perceived benefits of group activities (music and other groups)

	Music groups		Other groups	
	Mean*	SD**	Mean*	SD**
I really enjoy taking part in group activities	3.73	.45	3.43	.50
Participation in group activities helps me to remain socially active	3.51	.55	3.31	.58
Participation in group activities is one way in which I remain involved in the community	3.36	.61	3.38	.55
Participating in group activities has helped to reduce the effects of stress in my life	3.32	.62	3.27	.57
Participating in group activities has given me an opportunity to show others what I can do	3.17	.75	3.17	.66
Participating in group activities has given me an opportunity to help other people	2.97	.69	3.19	.59

*1 = strongly disagree; 4 = strongly agree.
**SD (standard deviation) refers to the range of scores; values less than 1 indicate relatively small variation in responses, in this case.

Rather, these findings do suggest that there may be something special about music that makes it particularly salient with regard to supporting social and emotional wellbeing. Music has the possibility of evoking powerful memories and thus bringing the past together with the present (Zanini and Leao, 2006). 'In this way, the entire body is involved ... and much more than this, the entire life is, too' (Martinez, 2000: 202). The link between music and social bonding (Cross, 2009; Hagen and Bryant, 2003), as well as research concerned with links between music and emotion (Juslin and Sloboda, 2010), may also help to explain the relationship between engagement in group music-making and an enhanced sense of wellbeing.

When questioned in focus-groups about what was special about music as opposed to other activities, many Music for Life Project participants attributed positive benefits to the communicative power of music, as well as referring repeatedly to the joyful nature of music-making (Box 2.9).

> **BOX 2.9 COMMUNICATIVE AND JOYFUL MUSIC-MAKING**
>
> There is definitely something in performing in a group, equal with everyone … And you actually physically get a tingle when something is good and you know it's good. There is also that you can nearly communicate with each other, well, you can communicate with each other by looking at each other … as you get older I find that if you don't think about it it's all intuitive; it just happens.
>
> Music for Life Project participant, Electric guitar group
>
> I think music is therapy, you know. I think it can really pick you right up … There is joy in music … The singing and the participation I think is … I don't think you would get that with any other group, you know. It's a happiness thing, music, isn't it?
>
> Music for Life Project participant, Ukulele and guitar group

Summary

Do musical social networks contribute to subjective social and emotional wellbeing, in later life? The evidence presented in this chapter suggests that older people who became actively engaged in musical social networks remained connected to their community, developing new role relationships and salient emotional attachments. Music-making helped to support subjective wellbeing through providing a rich context where individuals collaborated in purposeful and valued activity, sharing in the joy of making music together.

Many specific social and emotional benefits have been identified and attributed to musical participation. These include reduced anxiety and alleviation of depression, emotional self-regulation, and communication. Musical engagement has been linked with increased confidence, creative expression, reconnection with the past, as well as contributing to feelings of accomplishment and empowerment. In addition to a wealth of qualitative data, quantitative measures of wellbeing suggest that musical groups are particularly powerful contexts for sustaining social and emotional wellbeing, through the Third and Fourth Ages.

Chapter 3

Music-making and cognitive wellbeing

This chapter considers the cognitive benefits for older people of making music. It outlines the value placed on music by older people, discusses naturally occurring changes in the brain as we age, and considers how neuroscientific research has demonstrated that brain plasticity continues throughout the lifespan. We outline the benefits of engagement with music in cases of extreme cognitive decline and in 'normal' ageing, providing examples from the Music for Life Project. The potential for creativity in later years and the role of music in reminiscence are discussed. We conclude by considering subjective perceptions of what might be essential in musical activities to maintain cognitive functioning alongside the evidence from psychological and neuroscientific studies.

Introduction

There has been much research focusing on the cognitive benefits of active engagement with music in children and young people (see Hallam, 2010 for a review). There has been much less research on the direct cognitive benefits of making music amongst older people, where the focus of research has tended to be on social-emotional and physical wellbeing. This is beginning to change, as neuroscience has demonstrated the plasticity of the brain throughout the lifespan (Altenmüller, 2003).

Despite the limited research on the cognitive benefits of making music, there is considerable evidence of the importance of music in the lives of older people (Laukka, 2007; Gembris, 2008; Hays and Minchiello, 2005). For instance, in a questionnaire study with 280 seniors aged 65–75, Laukka (2007) investigated the association between music listening behaviours, psychological wellbeing, and background variables. The findings showed that two thirds of the participants listened to music once or several times a day, suggesting that music is more important to those aged 65+ than to younger people, even those in the teenage years. In addition to using music as a means of changing mood, contemplating, and working through emotions, for older people it also seems to have a spiritual quality (Hays and Minchiello, 2005).

> Apart from the feeling that music brings to our heart, I love the feeling in my brain. I think it's a very positive experience – brings a lot of happiness and tranquillity, and feeling you are able to learn something you love.
>
> Jacintha, aged 75, Music for Life Project participant

Lifelong musical development

Lifespan psychology suggests that there is no dominant age period in terms of the regulation of development. It is constantly evolving with periods of gain, deterioration and stability throughout the lifespan (Baltes *et al.*, 2006). This is also the case for musical development (see also Chapter 5). Musical learning and changes in musical ability can occur at any point in an individual's lifetime (Gembris, 2006). Musical learning is related to the immediate opportunities that the individual has, but also the broader musical culture and historical context within which they live. For instance, the emergence of rock and pop music in the 1950s and 60s is likely to have strongly influenced the musical preferences, interests, activities, and identities of the generation whose formative years were during this period.

In a study with older amateur musicians, Gembris (2008) found that many had an interruption of nearly 20 years to their musical activities when family commitments interfered. Around the age of retirement more time was available to resume activities. The participants in the study were asked to assess the quality of their instrumental performance. Their best performance on an instrument was not necessarily located in childhood. Typically, it was identified in the first three decades of life or between the ages of 60 and 69. This challenges the widely held view that performance declines with increasing age. In addition, almost 30 per cent of the interviewed senior musicians (average age 71) reported that they currently had reached 90 to 100 per cent of their former best instrumental performance.

Decline in performance with age

Musical activities are affected by age-related changes in cognitive, sensory, and physiological functioning. In adulthood, there is a general decrease in sensorimotor speed and dexterity, a reduction in the sense of touch, and limitations on aspects of movement. These, along with a reduction in the speed of cognitive processing, can impact on instrumental playing. There is also a gradual decline in hearing, while singers experience problems with changes in the voice (Kline and Scialfa, 1996). However, there are wide individual differences in the onset of these age-related changes, in part related to the particular types of expertise which the individual has developed over time (Krampe, 1994). For instance, professional piano players have been shown to be less affected by a decline in finger dexterity than untrained amateurs. While the professionals showed typical age-related general decline in mental speed, in expertise-related measures like tapping tasks, finger sequencing and coordination, this was not the case. They had largely maintained their performance level, the critical factor being the practice they had invested in these skills, which they had continued over the lifespan (Krampe, 2006). What this demonstrates is that continued extensive activity in a domain in older age can maintain high levels of performance in that domain.

Extreme cognitive decline

The most extreme cognitive decline occurs in those with dementia. This is typically defined as a serious loss of global cognitive ability in a previously unimpaired person, beyond that which might be expected from 'normal' ageing. Dementia is not a single disease, but a set of signs and symptoms. The areas affected include memory, attention, language, and problem solving. Alongside these, about 20–30 per cent of people who have dementia also suffer from depression and about 20 per cent experience anxiety (Calleo and Stanley, 2008). Alzheimer's disease is the most common form of dementia. Although Alzheimer's disease develops differently for every individual, there are many common symptoms, the most common in the early stages being an inability to remember recent events. As the disease advances, symptoms can include confusion, irritability, aggression, mood swings, and problems with language and long term memory. Suggested ways of delaying cognitive symptoms have included mental stimulation, exercise, and a balanced diet (Waldemar *et al.*, 2007).

While active engagement with music cannot prevent dementia (some eminent musicians have had to cease performing because of it), there is some evidence that it may slightly reduce the risk. Verghese *et al.* (2003) carried out a study considering the impact of leisure activities on the risk of dementia. Four hundred and eighty-eight English speaking participants aged 75–85 were interviewed using a medical-history questionnaire. The findings demonstrated a significant association between a high level of participation in leisure activities and a reduction in the risk of developing dementia. Participation in an activity for one day per week was associated with a reduction of 7 per cent of the risk. This finding remained robust even after adjustment for potential confounding variables such as age, sex, educational level, the presence or absence of chronic medical illnesses, and baseline cognitive status. Playing board games, a musical instrument, and dancing were all associated with a lower risk of dementia.

For those with moderate or severe dementia, group musical activities have been used in care homes as therapy to facilitate reminiscence and engagement (see Pavlicevic, 2012). There seem to be some benefits of listening to music or participating in singing activities (Skingley and Vella-Burrows, 2010). Studies exploring the effects of music therapy interventions on psychological and biochemical measures in adults with Alzheimer's and related disorders have all found an improvement in psychological and behavioural symptoms (Kumar *et al.*, 1999; Suzuki *et al.*, 2004, 2007; Takahashi and Matsushita, 2006). However, no significant effects have been found on measures of intelligence, indicating that the effects are not addressing the underlying decline.

Svansdottir and Snaedel (2006) conducted a small controlled trial on the value of group singing for elderly patients with moderate to severe dementia. The intervention involved small groups of participants encouraged by a music therapist to sing and use instruments in 30-minute sessions, three times a week for six weeks. Activity disturbances were significantly reduced in the singing group over the six-week intervention. Also, combined scores for activity disturbances, aggressiveness, and anxiety showed a significant reduction. However these beneficial changes were not maintained after a four-week follow-up. The intervention was only effective while it was ongoing.

Similarly, Myskyja and Nord (2008) carried out a natural experiment in a nursing home for residents with dementia. When the music therapist took leave of absence musical activities in the home ceased and staff reported increased depression amongst residents. The return of the music therapist gave an opportunity to more formally assess the effects. A significant reduction in depression was found over a period of two months of twice-weekly group singing. The greatest improvements were amongst those residents with the highest levels of engagement with the singing.

There are also benefits of such interventions for those acting as care-givers. As one facilitator in the Music for Life Project reported, one participant 'got her husband back' for an hour and a half a week 'because the music triggers something nothing else does. He doesn't speak the rest of the time but in this group he will sing the songs he knows and then he is more alert.'

Overall, the evidence suggests that engagement with music can, in the short term, ameliorate some symptoms of dementia, particularly those related to emotional and social behaviour. However, it does not offer long-term benefits for cognition amongst those with dementia, and systematic reviews of group singing have not identified it as an effective intervention in that sense (Hulme *et al.*, 2008; O'Connor *et al.*, 2009a, b). Notwithstanding this, engagement with music can alleviate symptoms and contribute to quality of life (Morrison and Clift, 2012a; Prickett, 2003; Vella-Burrows, 2012; Vella-Burrows and Hancox, 2012):

> Singing is integral to the life quality of those who are in progressive dementia and their care-givers. It functions to provide islands of arousal, awareness, familiarity, comfort, community, and success like nothing else can ... it is accessible to a wide array of individuals ... and can include persons across cultures and socioeconomic strata.
>
> (Clair, 2000: 93)

The benefits of making music on cognition in ageing

Although there is relatively little research on the cognitive benefits of engaging with music in later life, many have proposed extensive benefits of engaging with learning more generally. Learning has been advocated as a means for empowering individuals, supporting independence, developing skills and competency, and contributing to sustained personal fulfilment and wellbeing (Glendenning and Battersby, 1990; Dench and Regan, 2000; Withnall, 2010). The UK Government Office for Science (2008) Foresight Project report coined the term 'mental capital', referring to cognitive and emotional resources, social skills, and resilience in the face of stress. This report suggested that continued engagement in learning was one significant way in which mental capital amongst older people could be unlocked and sustained, protecting against cognitive decline, depression, and anxiety amongst the ageing population.

Certainly, the participants in both music and control groups in the Music for Life Project believed that active engagement with group activities supported their continuing cognitive functioning. In responding to a series of statements, all either agreed or strongly agreed that participation in group activities provided an opportunity for regular mental activity, that acquiring new skills and knowledge was a very satisfying experience, and that participation in group activities was intellectually stimulating. Ninety per cent considered continuing lifelong learning to be a priority, while 83 per cent indicated that participation gave them the opportunity to show others what they could do.

Such research as has been conducted relating to lifelong learning in music has shown that those who are actively engaged in making music have enhanced cognitive and psychomotor performance and a higher level of life satisfaction than might be expected. For instance, Moser (2003) studied 120 musically active individuals in the United States and, in comparisons with average demographic data, music offered a range of cognitive and quality-of-life benefits.

Studies with instrumentalists have also revealed cognitive benefits. For instance, Gembris (2008) carried out a questionnaire study with members of senior amateur orchestras with an average age of 71 years and found a range of benefits of music-making. While these were generally related to wellbeing, music was seen as helping them to cope and deal with difficult situations, clearly requiring a range of cognitive skills. Participants in singing activities have also commented on the way that singing stimulates cognitive capacity including attention, concentration, memory, and learning (Clift *et al.*, 2008).

Older adults (aged 60–85) receiving individualized piano lessons over a six month period in an experimental study carried out by Bugos *et al.* (2007) showed significant improvement in attention, concentration, and planning, compared with controls. The tuition seemed to have had transfer effects on general cognitive measures that had not been specifically trained. The authors suggested that as the performer actively allocates attentional resources to musical passages the integration of multiple networks through repeated practice is reinforced and transferred to other cognitive domains. For these benefits to be maintained regular practice and tuition is needed, as decline followed when the activities ceased. In a similar study with adult piano students aged 24–90, average age 51, Jutras (2006) also found musical skill-based improvements alongside those related to personal and social benefits.

A number of those participating in the Music for Life Project specifically mentioned that their engagement in music supported concentration and memory. For example, singing in parts, memorizing music, and the concentration required for listening to new music and taking part in ensemble playing were perceived as stimulating cognitive challenges that contributed to feeling active and alert. Progression and a sense of accomplishment when goals had been attained were important in supporting motivation and commitment. Being able to remember songs also allowed participation by those who had visual impairment. For example, one interviewee commented on the need for her father to learn the words before attending his singing group, using a song sheet and magnifying glass, because he was now registered blind. Example responses are provided in Boxes 3.1 and 3.2.

Box 3.1 Cognitive benefits reported by those participating in making music

Concentration and memory

I feel samba and drum-kit are particularly good for the grey cells! I have to concentrate and remember.

I definitely feel that my concentration and memory have improved since joining. It's good for memory and concentration and is relaxing except when some phrases are difficult to master, then it becomes a challenge.

I've got a friend that's got that [Alzheimer's] ... it's a marvellous thing with everything he's got wrong with him, he can't remember this and he can't remember that, but ... I sang a couple of songs and he joined in, and he was word perfect. ... if you sing music to them and they know it, they'll sing it because that seems to stick in their minds, which is a wonderful thing.

Music for Life Project participants

Maintains an active mind

It keeps my mind active and I have felt better emotionally after singing sessions. I do think that being involved in music definitely keeps you young. ... Because, like I am saying, you are using this mental ability all the time and that's got to be good, hasn't it?

Music for Life Project participants

Maintains intellectual interest

The music class has encouraged me to listen to classical music and go to BBC recordings. All the classes I attend have encouraged me and kept me from feeling bored.
It keeps me active, alert, and organized. It allows me to use and build on previous experience. It introduces me to new ideas and extends my appreciation of different musical genres.

Music for Life Project participants

Maintains brain activity

> It is exercising the brain. That keeps the brain working and I think that it is quite good for flexibility of the fingers, the concentration ...

> You have to concentrate really hard and, you know, when you stop working you don't do things like that and you tend not to concentrate on stuff. So, it's very good to keep your brain going.

> Music for Life Project participants

BOX 3.2 PERCEPTIONS OF HOW MUSIC CAN BENEFIT COGNITION

Excerpts from the focus group discussion with those participating in the Samba class

> I thought I would never pick it up at first, I would never get used to this but you gradually get into the way of it.

> It keeps the brain ticking over because you've got to have your wits about you, otherwise you do 'boom' when you shouldn't have had. And that's it, it is great fun.

> The teachers make things very easy for us to learn and build it up very slowly ... And we play different instruments so we are not just playing the same instrument all the time. We move around.

> But it's good for you, absolutely! And I think the thing about keeping your brain ticking is really good ...

> I am at a singing group ... which does world music and I found that my sense of rhythm has improved terrifically when I am singing from what I have learned in the drumming. It's improved my singing, because I am able to deal with the rhythms from abroad much, much better than I could before.

> Music for Life Project participants

Music and reminiscence

Throughout the lifespan music has a role in reminiscence. As we age this seems to take on increasing importance, perhaps because reminiscence can support us as we adapt to change, deal with stress, validate our lives, boost self-esteem, and evaluate the quality of our lives (Clair, 1996). Music is particularly powerful in supporting retrieval from long-term memory. For example, interviews with 38 individuals aged 60–98 revealed that music evoked many vivid memories of events and experiences (Hays and Minichiello, 2005). Interviewees described how music was used to link and review their life experiences and its meanings, and the importance of 'this gift' in their life. Some of the memories evoked were not pleasant and some music was deliberately avoided because of its negative associations.

In the Music for Life Project, one facilitator reported how the group's memories of life experiences were triggered by listening to or talking about music. There was also a benefit for the facilitator who could include the memories as a resource for the group.

> It's a great thing to tap into the group's ideas and memories especially. All of the group have got fabulous recollections of music and how it's been part of their lives and that's where a lot of the inspiration comes from ... given the combined experience of this group, it seems like someone has always got a story, whatever we listen to there'll be some connection. We had some this morning. Two of the group had been to New Orleans. Also when we did the Danube a couple of weeks ago, a couple of people had been to places on the Danube and one had been on a river cruise, and she'd obviously had a wonderful holiday, it was like 40 years ago or something. We did a topic on New York, it's not always places but sometimes it is, and Leonard Bernstein was part of that. John in the group said 'Oh I know Leonard Bernstein', or he'd met him. ... Tell us the story.
>
> Facilitator, Music for Life Project

Thus, through using music as a tool for reminiscence, some facilitators provided participants with opportunities to make significant links with their personal stories and to contribute meaningfully to (musical) social situations. A case-study example is provided in Box 3.3.

Box 3.3 Case study of music-making and reminiscence

Martha engaged in music-making because music brought back significant memories from her past. She was born in 1919 and lived on her own in a flat provided by sheltered housing accommodation in East London. A care-giver visited her twice a day, and her son and one of her grandchildren visited her every evening. During her interview Martha indicated that she liked the song 'Mamma Mia' which was rehearsed during the sessions. She also liked opera, her favourite aria was 'Nessun Dorma' and she enjoyed watching André Rieu from Vienna on the TV. With regard to the things she enjoyed the most about the project, Martha referred to playing small percussion instruments and singing, and added that she would like the group to sing 'Champagne Charlie' because this song reminded her of her late husband and her favourite singer Gracie Fields.

> He used to sing it. [She then sings 'Champagne Charlie is my name …'] I can't remember the other words. The other song is 'I am Burlington Bertie, I rise at ten thirty' [she sings these lines]. They are all Maxy Miller's … 'Daisy Daisy' [she sings that]. Have you ever heard of Gracie Fields … She used to sing 'Daisy' … She always used to sing 'Daisy Daisy'. And years and years ago when I was in my teens I was in service and I was working in Belsize Park. I looked after the house, you know. And he was a barrister, the people that I worked for and the garden in the house where I worked in Hampstead was attached to the garden of another house that was in Finchley Road. And I found out that Gracie Fields … she used to go in the garden singing because she used to have a lot of children.
>
> My dear husband, he had Alzheimer's. So I would remind him and he would remind me of songs I couldn't remember. At his funeral they played 'Champagne Charlie is my name.' I lost him just before Christmas. He was 94. Seventy years we have been married.
>
> Martha, Music for Life Project participant

Martha participated in the musical activities because she liked listening to music, particularly opera. This provided her with an opportunity to remember songs of her times and songs that her husband sang to her. Music participation had a positive impact on her emotional wellbeing, especially during a period of distress after her husband's death.

Creativity

There has been little research into creativity in older age. Cohen (2009) argues that humans have inner drives that foster psychological growth throughout the life cycle. He describes four phases that relate to ageing: a mid-life re-evaluation phase (generally from the early 40s to the late 50s, when plans and actions are shaped by a sense of crisis or quest); a liberation phase (generally from the mid-50s to the mid-70s where plans and actions are shaped by a sense of personal freedom); a summing-up phase (usually from the late 60s to 80s, where plans and actions are shaped by the desire to find meaning, as individuals look back and reflect) and an encore phase (developing in the late 70s, where plans and actions are shaped by the desire to reaffirm major life themes, explore variations on those themes and attend to unfinished business). Cohen proposes that as individuals progress through these phases creativity may increase and that the arts can support this process and play a major contribution in supporting wellbeing. An example of this was seen in the Music for Life Project. This is set out in Box 3.4 (also see Varvarigou *et al.*, 2013).

> **BOX 3.4 CASE-STUDY OF CREATIVITY AND SELF-EXPRESSION**
> Rick, born in 1918, saw the music sessions as an opportunity to create songs with a special meaning for him and share them with the group during the music sessions. Rick's favourite music was songs by Joe Longthorne, which he played as background to the face-to-face interview. Rick led a very active life. The music sessions started one year after his computer classes had ceased and this pleased him as it gave him the opportunity to remain active and enjoy social interactions.
>
> > I would attend more to anything like that. Life can be pretty boring in a place like that. I mean, I am out every day. I don't stay in but a lot of people don't move and there is nothing in their life. They look at television. But when

they come [the musicians], we are talking and laughing and singing and it's great.

Rick, Music for Life Project participant

However, joining the music session turned out to be more of a self-exploratory journey for Rick. In the interview Rick said that what he enjoyed most about the music sessions was playing the electric piano and understanding the lyrics of the songs. He also talked about his life; the fact that he had never played any musical instrument – unlike his siblings and father who all played the piano. During his years in prison, joining the choir, despite being a 'growler', was an opportunity to avoid heavy chores and to belong to a group, 'gang' in prison language. Rick asked the music facilitator for private tuition in creating song lyrics. This released his creative spirit. During the first term of the project the music facilitator encouraged the group to work collaboratively to create lyrics and short riffs or melodies that could lead to a song. This idea inspired Rick to secretly start writing his own lyrics. The facilitator remembered how Rick initially lacked the confidence to claim ownership of his song and how later on, after the song was very well received by the group, he became more confident and proud, and made plans to create more songs.

Rick created the lyrics to a song called 'I'm Sorry Now' that talked about his regret for the hurt caused to his wife when he was sentenced to a term in prison. Having experienced success as a songwriter, Rick's second song 'In the Middle of a Kiss' was created several months after the first one. It was much longer in duration and talked about successful love that 'passed the test of time' (see Box 3.5).

During the second term of the music programme Rick asked the music facilitators to show him how to play some chords on the electric keyboard so that he could accompany the rest of the group when they sang or played percussion instruments. When asked, at the end of the project, what might make the music activity he was part of even more enjoyable, Rick replied that he 'really enjoyed piano [keyboard] music', probably indicating that he would like to engage with playing the keyboard more in the future. When asked if there had been any changes in his life in the last six months that had affected his taking part in the group activities, Rick replied that he had 'tried to make verse', demonstrating more confidence than earlier in talking about his creative activities.

> When this project started in October last year I didn't think it would last. I thought it was just a whim and it probably wouldn't last and we would all get bored of it. But as it turned out it was very encouraging and we enjoyed every minute and we ran through until May this year. We never missed a meeting. We enjoyed it immensely. Z. [principal music facilitator] would give us every encouragement and especially with me. I wrote the words to a song and I didn't think it was much good but she rather liked it and we have been playing it in the Barbican. I am very pleased, I am very happy! Everybody enjoyed it.
>
> Rick, Music for Life Project participant

For Rick, involvement in musical activities was not only an opportunity to socialize and keep active. Ultimately, it was a cathartic experience that offered an avenue for self-expression, creativity, and a way to resolve emotional tensions with memories from his past.

Box 3.5 Rick's songs

'I'm Sorry Now'

> *I paid for the pain I've caused you*
> *I paid in so many ways*
> *Why should my moments of madness*
> *Bring you a lifetime of sadness?*
> *I'm sorry now, but darling I vow,*
> *I'll die if we ever part*
> *Would you please take me back some day?*
> **Chorus**
> *Take me back, take me back,*
> * take me back some day (×2)*

'In the Middle of a Kiss'

> *In the middle of a kiss*
> *We stumbled into Paradise*

> *In the twinkle of an eye*
> *I knew that you were mine*
> *We didn't comprehend*
> > *our love would ever end*
> *Just the way it began*
> *in the middle of a kiss*
> **Chorus**
> *In the middle of a kiss (×4)*
> **Verse 2**
> *They said it wouldn't last*
> *We'd left it in the past they'd say*
> *We passed the test of time*
> > *our love was ever strong*
> *We didn't comprehend*
> > *our love would ever end*
> *Just the way it began*
> > *in the middle of a kiss*
> **Chorus**
>
> Rick, Music for Life Project participant

The mechanisms that underpin the wider cognitive benefits of music

The participants in the Music for Life Project spoke of the importance of being challenged, although it was important for challenge to be balanced with enjoyment (see also Chapter 6). Singing in parts, focusing on the minutiae of playing and performance, making progress, and having high standards were all seen as part of the challenge. Where repertoire or teaching approaches were felt to be childish or lacking in strategies for progression the participants were critical. At times the facilitators had to make difficult judgements as to how much to challenge participants in sessions as opposed to offering more familiar activities and repertoire. However, when balance was achieved, the activities were extremely appealing to older learners:

> There is no point in doing something you can already do. The fun is coming across something and thinking 'I am never gonna be able to do this, but I am going to try!' and then suddenly you can [do it].
>
> Pam, Music for Life Project, guitar group

Being successful in meeting the challenges posed led to a great sense of achievement that in itself was enjoyable, stimulating and rewarding. Musical performances were also important, providing goals to aim for, and a focus for the learning. Recollections of performances were dominant in group discussions. The participants remembered significant moments and made reflective comments relating to a sense of relaxation, achievement, collective effort, and the 'buzz' that they had felt during performances. It was also evident that those who performed regularly had become quite self-critical.

The subjective accounts from participants in the Music for Life Project, of making progress, learning, enhanced concentration, and improved memory are reflected in a range of studies with musicians of all ages and at all levels of expertise. All musical performance requires the individual to have control over the focus of attention (Duke *et al.*, 2011), to manage the integration of a range of sensory and motor skills (Münte *et al.*, 2002), and carefully plan and monitor performance (Palmer and Drake, 1997). The development of these skills leads to changes in the brain, the greater the length of time engaged with making music the greater the change.

Comparisons between the brains of professional musicians and non-musicians have demonstrated differences in the auditory and sensorimotor areas required for musical processing (Schneider *et al.*, 2002; Zatorre *et al.*, 1998). There are also differences in the frontal cortex of musicians and non-musicians. This is the area concerned with the regulation of attention (Gaser and Schlaug, 2003; Sluming *et al.*, 2002). While it might be expected that musical training would benefit auditory processing that may transfer to other auditory tasks, it seems that there are also transfer effects involving the regulation of attention and working memory (Parberry-Clark *et al.*, 2009; Schellenberg and Moreno, 2010). The core functions involved in musical activities are executive functions. These are predominantly located in the frontal cortex. Musical engagement increases grey-matter density in the frontal brain areas involved in controlling musical practice tasks (e.g. Hyde *et al.*, 2009). Listening to music, performing music, and moving to music engage regions throughout the cortex, subcortex, and cerebellum (see Perez and Zatorre, 2005).

There has been little research into the relationship between music training and cognitive abilities in later adulthood. There is evidence that older amateur musicians outperform non-musicians in a variety of aural tasks (Parbery-Clark *et al.*, 2011; Zendel and Alain, 2012) but evidence of transfer to other tasks has been less consistent. In some cases, older adults with high levels of musical training have performed better than their musically untrained counterparts in cognitive control tasks involving nonverbal memory and cognitive flexibility (Hanna-Pladdy and MacKay, 2011) but the findings have been inconsistent (Hanna-Pladdy and Gajewski, 2012).

Amer *et al.* (2013) studied late middle-aged to older professional musicians and non-musicians with similar general education, vocabulary, and overall health. They compared the performance of the two groups on a range of auditory tasks, visuospatial memory span, cognitive control processes and a composite measure of cognitive control. In general, although there were exceptions in relation to some verbal tasks, the musicians outperformed the non-musicians in the auditory tasks. This is supported by neurophysiological research demonstrating that relative to non-musicians, older musicians show enhanced attention-dependent neural activity associated with isolating simultaneously occurring sounds (Zendel and Alain, 2013). The musicians' advantage in auditory control seems to be specific to pitch identification. In the far-transfer tasks, musicians showed advantages in visuospatial span and in many aspects of cognitive control.

This visuospatial advantage may stem, in part, from professional musicians' greater experience and proficiency with sight-reading and consequent memory enhancement for complex patterns (Goolsby, 1994). The musicians performed better in a reading task which assessed the ability to control irrelevant visual and textual cues while reading text. The musicians were faster than non-musicians in the high-interference condition involving irrelevant words. They omitted fewer relevant words and included fewer irrelevant words. Overall, they exercised better control than non-musicians when confronted with visually or spatially distracting events. This suggests that they preserved inhibitory regulation (Hasher *et al.*, 1999). The findings from this research suggest that high levels of musical expertise and sustained engagement in music-making are associated with the enhancement or preservation of cognitive-control abilities in older adults.

Further evidence that musical practice involves the frontal cortex in elderly adults has been provided by Sluming *et al.* (2002) who demonstrated that musicians continuing to practise beyond 60 years of age showed less or no degeneration of grey-matter density in the frontal cortex. Practising a musical instrument seems to prevent deterioration of executive functions involving monitoring and planning. Long-term musical practice seems to be sufficiently demanding cognitively to mitigate age-related decline. It may be that these effects can be explained by improved neural efficiency in general control networks, allowing cognitively active individuals to better cope with age-related neural changes.

Music's reliance on the auditory system may also be important in reducing neural decline in executive functions. The auditory system has been shown to be highly efficient in comparison with other systems, possibly owing to its time-ordered nature and the temporal organization of functional skills (learning, language, attention, memory, executive function). The auditory scaffolding hypothesis states that due to this complex temporal organization, experiences that are auditory may provide scaffolding for the rehabilitation or development of general cognitive abilities (Conway *et al.*, 2009). Thaut (2005) also showed that the temporal organization of music can be utilized to improve cognitive functions. Engagement in music during a cognitive task facilitates synchronized firing of neurons resulting in faster and more efficient learning. Improved neurological timing has been demonstrated with electroencephalogram (EEG) measures of brainwave activity where musical stimuli evoke more synchronized firings in alpha and gamma bandwidths (Thaut *et al.*, 2005).

The physical effort associated with regular practice and performance may also be relevant to the maintenance of executive functions in older age as there is evidence that physical fitness interventions have demonstrable positive cognitive consequences in older adults, especially for tasks involving cognitive control (Colcombe and Kramer, 2003).

The pleasure of performing in temporal synchrony with others is also likely to have wide-ranging consequences for wellbeing and overall function (McNeill, 1995). Indeed, the enjoyment derived from all musical activities activates dopaminergic neurons that are powerful aids to attention and learning (Keitz *et al.*, 2003). Dopamine is critical to the neurobiology of reward learning, for instance, addiction to heroin, alcohol, cocaine, and nicotine activates dopaminergic systems. The activation of dopaminergic neurons may account for the intense pleasure (peak experiences) of some musical experiences and support ongoing motivation to engage with music.

Summary

There has been much research into the cognitive benefits of active engagement with music in children and young people, but less on the direct cognitive benefits for older people making music. Despite this, there is considerable evidence of the importance of music in the lives of older people. Musical learning and changes in musical ability can occur at any point in an individual's lifetime. While there are age-related changes in cognitive, sensory and physiological functioning, continued extensive activity in a domain in older age can maintain high levels of performance in that domain. In extreme cases of cognitive decline, engagement with music can enhance general wellbeing and through reminiscence stimulate memory, but there is no long-term impact on cognitive functions.

For 'normal' ageing, such research that has been carried out has shown that those who are actively engaged in making music have enhanced cognitive and psychomotor performance and a higher level of life satisfaction. This was supported by the evidence from the Music for Life Project. Music also provides opportunities for creativity in older age and supports the maintenance of cognitive functions largely through its impact on executive functions in the frontal cortex. The involvement of physical activity in making music and the rewards it offers also play an important role in maintaining executive function (the physical benefits of music-making are explored in Chapter 4). Overall, there is increasing interest in the cognitive benefits of music-making in the Third and Fourth Ages, alongside a growing body of research supporting the view that music-making in later life has great potential to contribute to sustained cognitive vitality.

Chapter 4

Music-making and physical wellbeing

This chapter sets out the rationale for the links between music, psychological wellbeing, and good health. We consider how music can impact on health, including its role in reducing stress, anxiety, and pain, and its impact on the immune system, lung functions, speech impairments, mobility and motor coordination, and general health. Participants in the Music for Life Project reported respiratory benefits, physical exercise, and increased joint-mobility. Singing in particular was perceived as having a direct benefit for physical health, through lung use and oxygenation of the blood. The physical nature of some musical activities was supported by warm-up exercises such as stretching and controlled breathing. The chapter concludes by considering new approaches to the role of music in health promotion, including the concept of 'health musicking' (Bonde, 2011) and 'community music therapy', which differ from community music in that they focus primarily on the needs and potential of participants with health problems.

Introduction

The role of music in health and healing has been recognized for more than 30,000 years. It is referred to in the Bible and the historical writings of ancient civilizations in Egypt, China, India, Greece, and Rome. Music Therapy as a profession developed in the United States following the two World Wars. Music was used to relieve the perception of pain of those with severe injuries and medical staff noted the positive psychological, physiological, cognitive, and emotional benefits to patients. Since then, with the increasingly easy availability of music through technological innovations, individuals have more frequently used music to manage their own moods and emotions (DeNora, 2000, 2007). Recently, there has been a surge of scientific interest in trying to understand the ways that music can impact on wellbeing and physical health and the extent of the possible benefits.

> I find singing in a group quite magical. I have experienced it in various groups on and off for around 13 years and I am sure it

> helps with enjoyment and physical wellbeing. It has helped me extremely in times of great personal difficulties.
>
> Judith, aged 79, Music for Life Project

As we saw in Chapter 2, the main benefits of active participation in making music seem to relate to social and personal wellbeing. However, there is increasingly compelling evidence indicating that mind-body interactions are crucial for good physical health. Psychological factors play a causal role in many illnesses (Pelletier, 1992; Bekkouche *et al.*, 2011) and can affect the speed and extent of recovery. Emotions impact on health and can also play a role in clinical outcomes (Leventhal and Patrick-Miller, 2000). They may also indirectly influence health-related behaviours (Diefenbach *et al.*, 2008). Overall, there is compelling evidence that positive emotions are associated with better health and health behaviours.

Music has a very powerful impact on our emotions (see Chapter 2). Its impact on psychological wellbeing and subsequently good health is largely, although not exclusively, through the emotions it evokes, which can be wide ranging (for a review see Juslin and Sloboda, 2010). Panksepp and Bernatzky (2002) suggest that the way music elicits emotions and changes moods is underpinned by its stimulation of the autonomic nervous system. They argue that musically induced activations involve cortical and sub-cortical neural networks in the human brain that are associated with endocrine systems and homeostatic changes in these systems. Bodily responses related to emotion include changes in dopamine, serotonin, cortisol, endorphin, and oxytocin levels (see van Eck *et al.*, 1996). These can all affect physical health. Results from a range of experimental, observation, and animal studies support this (e.g. Kubzansky 2009). These issues will be considered further, later in the chapter.

Juslin *et al.* (2010) suggest that there are seven mechanisms through which music affects emotions:

- brain stem reflexes (pre-wired responses to the simple acoustic characteristics of music such as volume and speed) (Sokolov 1963)
- rhythmic entrainment (gradual adjustment of an internal body rhythm (e.g. heart rate) towards an external rhythm) (Harrer and Harrer, 1977)
- evaluative conditioning (regular pairing of a piece of music with other positive or negative stimuli) (Blair and Shimp, 1992)
- emotional contagion (perception of emotionally relevant expression in the music that is then copied) (Lundqvist *et al.*, 2009)
- visual imagery (images with emotional qualities are evoked by the music) (Osborne 1981)

- episodic memory (music evoking the memory of particular events) (Baumgartner, 1992)
- musical expectancy (a musical event violates, delays, or confirms the expectations of listeners leading to feelings of tension and suspense or release and relaxation (Meyer, 1956).

The specific ways in which the emotions are invoked depends on complex interactions between the nature of the music, the individual, and the context. Musical preferences play a major part in the nature of the impact of music on the emotions. The more familiar we are with particular pieces of music or genres the more we tend to like them (North and Hargreaves, 2008). Thus, exposure to music modifies liking. Much of this is determined by early experiences of music. In practice, this means that music that is pleasurable for some individuals may be unpleasant for others. Research on the impact of music on health has shown that the most positive benefits occur when individuals are able to select the music that they listen to (Mitchell and MacDonald, 2006). Despite this there are some musical characteristics that tend to have a relatively consistent effect on arousal levels, arousal being closely related to emotion. Quiet, slow music tends to lead to a lowering of arousal levels, while fast and loud music tends to be viewed as arousing (North and Hargreaves, 2008). There is also evidence that some kinds of music may have negative effects on health-related factors. Evers and Suhr (2000) investigated the short-term effects of musical excerpts on serum concentrations of prolactin, ACTH (adrenocorticotropic hormone), and serotonin in healthy adult listeners. Serotonin contributes to feelings of wellbeing. Some excerpts were characterized as pleasant (Brahms's Third Symphony, Opus 90), others as unpleasant (Penderecki's 'Threnos', which is in part composed in quarter-tones, making the dissonance of the music very prominent). Listening to 'Threnos' reduced concentrations of serotonin, suggesting a negative impact on wellbeing.

In addition to the impact that music can have on emotions it has also long been known that listening to music has a wide range of physiological effects on the human body, including changes in heart rate, respiration, blood pressure, skin conductivity, skin temperature, muscle tension, and biochemical responses (see Kreutz and Lotze, 2008).

As noted in Chapter 3, older people listen to a great deal of music, even more than those in the adolescent years (Laukka, 2007). The participants in the Music for Life Project also reported engaging in a wide range of musical activities. Ninety-six per cent reported listening to recorded music, 81 per cent listened to live music, 80 per cent had music playing in the background when they were completing other tasks. Seventy-nine per cent reported singing at home, and 49 per cent practised at home. They played a wide range of instruments and had a wide range of musical preferences (see Hallam *et al.*, 2012 for details). Hays and Minchiello (2005: 443) in their study with 52 people aged 60–98 years reported that 'many participants felt music was the key to feeling a sense of wellbeing and good health regardless of their particular personal medical condition'. Music accompanying daily activities led participants to feel happier, more relaxed, satisfied, and secure. Given the extent to which music plays a part in older people's lives, and the evidence of its impact on wellbeing (see Chapter 2), we might therefore expect that it would also have benefits for their health.

Next in this chapter we set out illustrative examples from the literature relating to the impact of music on health and how this occurs. Overall, psychological processes associated with musical experiences lead to changes in the hormonal systems of brain and body. The nervous and endocrine systems often act together to regulate the physiological processes of the human body. Music can impact on these systems. Empirical approaches over the last twenty years have begun to adopt a psychoneuroendocrine approach that examines the effects of musical stimulation using a range of measures (Kreutz *et al.*, 2012). In addition, there is evidence that active engagement with music may impact on issues relating to lung function, language, mobility, and fine motor coordination. Much of this research has not been undertaken with older people but with a wider adult population. However, there is no reason to suppose that the effects would not apply to older people.

Music, stress and anxiety

Health problems occurring as a result of long-term stress and recurring negative emotions are well documented in the literature (depression's links with cancer, anger with cardiovascular disease (see Davidson *et al.*, 2003; Steptoe, 1997). Stress can also reduce the speed of recovery. Engaging with music has been shown to be able to induce relaxation and reduce stress. Certainly, individuals report that music helps them to relax. For instance, a study in Sweden using a representative sample of the Swedish population found that 78 per cent reported that they listened to music at least once every day and that one of the reasons for doing so was that it helped them to relax (Juslin *et al.*, 2011). Using music as opposed to other means of relaxation was reported as being more effective because it was possible to tailor it to personal taste and it was available at any time or location.

Cortisol levels have been used in music-related studies as a psychophysiological measure of stress. Significant reductions in cortisol have been found in healthy adults when they listen to classical choral (Kreutz *et al.*, 2004), meditative (Mockel *et al.*, 1994), and folk music (Fukui and Yamashita, 2003). However, not all music has this effect. Significant increases in cortisol have been noted in listeners who are exposed to techno music (Gerra *et al.*, 1998) and upbeat pop and rock music (Brownley *et al.*, 1995).

Singing and other participatory musical activities can also bring about changes in cortisol levels. Beck *et al.* (2000) observed decreases of cortisol of 30 per cent, on average, in members of a professional choir during a rehearsal, although there was a 37 per cent increase during a performance. Music stimulation has also been found to have an effect on cortisol levels in the context of tango dancing. Murcia *et al.* (2009) observed that the presence of music during dance led to decreases of cortisol levels. A similar effect was not observed in the presence or absence of a dance partner.

In clinical contexts exposure to music has been shown to reduce cortisol levels during medical treatment (e.g. Le Roux *et al.*, 2007). For instance, in pre-operative settings in hospitals where patients are often suffering from complex sets of conditions including pain, anxiety, distress, and even aggressive non-compliance, meta-analytic analyses have demonstrated that music can help to reduce anxiety (Spintge 2012). Conrad *et al.* (2007) played critically ill patients slow movements from Mozart's piano sonatas and found that the use of this music significantly reduced the amount of sedative drugs needed to achieve the degree of sedation required comparable to controls who received a standard therapy. In the music group plasma concentrations of growth hormone increased whereas those of interleukin-6 (a component of the immune system) and adrenaline decreased. In addition, significantly lower levels of blood pressure and heart rate indicated reductions in systemic stress. Overall, the calming music activated neurohumoral pathways associated with psychophysiological sedation.

Grape *et al.* (2003) observed significant increases of oxytocin, which plays a fundamental role in social behaviours, in both professional and amateur singers after a singing lesson. In a clinical context, Nelson *et al.* (2008) compared the effects of music listening on the first day after coronary surgery in groups of patients with and without music stimulation. Oxytocin level increases were observed in those receiving musical stimulation, while decreases were found in the other participants.

Music listening in combination with guided imagery has been found to lead to significant reductions of the β-endorphin, which the body uses to numb or dull pain (McKinney *et al.*, 1997). However, music listening or guided imagery alone did not have this effect. Vollert *et al.* (2003) delivered special relaxation music to coronary patients during rehabilitation and found significant decreases of β-endorphin during physical exercises, suggesting that the music compensated in some way for the need for the natural pain relief. In addition, systolic blood pressure, anxiety, and worry were also reduced. Decreases were not significant in patients who performed the exercises without music. Gerra *et al.* (1998) extended these observations by showing that listening to upbeat techno music led to increases of endorphin levels in groups of healthy adults, suggesting that upbeat music differed from more relaxing music, in that it did not have the effect of compensating for β-endorphins.

Music can assist in pain reduction, speeding-up recovery time and reducing drug dosages by up to 50 per cent (e.g. Spintge and Droh, 1992; Spintge 2012). The most effective music in this context is that selected by the participants themselves (Mitchell and McDonald, 2006).

Music and the immune system

Some studies have assessed the impact of music on the immune system by taking samples of secretory immunoglobulin A (sIgA) in saliva, before and after musical activity. sIgA is often used as an indicator of the local immune system in the upper respiratory tract and the first line of defence against bacterial and viral infections. Reported increases point to enhanced immune-system activity after singing (e.g. Beck *et al.*, 2000; Kuhn 2002; Kreutz *et al.*, 2004; Beck, Gottfried, Hall, Cisler and Bozeman 2006). Kreutz *et al.* (2004) found that one hour rehearsing choral music in an amateur choral society led to significant increases in sIgA, but no such increase over time was found in those listening to choral music. However, McCraty and colleagues (1996) investigated the effects of listening to relaxing music and generating a positive emotional state on sIgA in healthy adults. The findings showed that combined these led to increases of sIgA concentrations, although rock or 'new-age' music had no effects. Kuhn (2002) in a study exploring active drumming or singing compared with watching a live performance found there was a more pronounced effect on those actively participating in making music. What seems to be emerging from this area of research is that there are positive relationships between making and listening to music and changes in sIgA (Beck *et al.*, 2000, 2006).

Lung function

Several studies have investigated the hypothesis that singing has a beneficial effect on aspects of breathing. Overall, the findings are mixed (see Clift, 2012). For instance, Schorr-Lesnick *et al.* (1985), compared singers with instrumentalists (adults aged 25–83) and reported no difference in pulmonary function between participants in choir, string, percussion, and wind ensembles. Studies of patients with chronic pulmonary diseases have also had mixed results, with some research into singing showing improvements compared with controls (Bonilha *et al.*, 2009), while some has shown limited impact (Lord *et al.*, 2010). Despite this, those participating in singing activities often report that the singing has exercised body systems through the physical exertion involved, especially the lungs (Clift *et al.*, 2008; Stacey *et al.*, 2002).

Speech impairments

Music can also play a therapeutic role in supporting improvement in speech impairments. Rhythmic cueing has been used to reduce speech rate and increase speech intelligibility in patients with severe dysarthria (problems with the muscles that support speech) due to traumatic brain injury, for instance, as a result of a stroke (Pilon *et al.*, 1998). Similar results have been found for increasing the intelligibility of the speech of patients with Parkinson's disease (Thaut *et al.*, 2001). Hays and Minichiello (2005) in an interview study found that music provided a means of communication with spouses, friends, or others where language based communication was restricted due to Parkinson's disease, dementia, or other illnesses affecting verbal communication.

Mobility and motor coordination

Most of the research on the benefits of music to mobility has focused on the use of rhythm (LaGasse and Thaut, 2012). Clinical evidence has shown that the use of external rhythmic auditory cueing can aid in the rehabilitation of motor movements, such as gait, in patients with Parkinson's disease, traumatic brain injury, spinal cord injury, and Huntington's disease.

Playing music can also be beneficial to rehabilitation for those who have partial paralysis resulting from stroke. Learning to play the piano or drums in a therapeutic setting can improve the quality, range, and speed of movements (Schneider *et al.*, 2007). While the motivational aspects of music may account for some of the gains, there is evidence of increased activation of the motor cortex and improved cortical connectivity (Altenmüller *et al.*, 2009). Patients who participated in therapeutic instrumental playing also demonstrated greater generalization of their motor skills to the home environment (Schneider *et al.*, 2007).

In relation to general psychomotor functions, starting at the age of 30, human physiological functions lose about 1 per cent of their efficiency every year. However, the body compensates so that these losses do not become apparent for some time. There is limited evidence that those who are musically active have improved psychomotor performance compared with averages derived from demographic data (Moser, 2003).

General health benefits of participation in making music

There has been relatively little research focusing on the general physical-health benefits of participation in music. There is some evidence of lower mortality rates amongst those who make music or sing in a choir (Byrgen *et al.*, 1996). In the UK, Hillman (2002) surveyed 75 participants who had participated in a community singing project since reaching the statutory retirement age. Long-term benefits attributed to participation in music included a lack of deterioration in physical health. In the USA, Cohen *et al.* (2006, 2007) carried out non-randomized controlled studies with 166 participants with a mean age of 80 who participated in 30 singing workshops and ten performances over one year. The intervention (chorale) group reported a higher overall rating of physical health, fewer doctor visits, less medication use, fewer instances of falls and other health problems in comparison with the control group, who had carried on with their usual activities and did not participate in the chorale. There was also evidence that morale was higher and there was less loneliness in the intervention group. The comparison group experienced a significant decline in total number of activities whereas the intervention group reported a trend towards increased activity. Cohen *et al.* argue that sense of control as well as social engagement were the most likely mechanisms responsible for the positive outcomes.

The Music for Life Project

The participants in the Music for Life project attributed some improvements in their physical health to their musical activities. These physical benefits included respiratory benefits, physical exercise and increased joint-mobility. Some participants mentioned that playing some of the instruments was physically hard work: 'It is quite hard work, too. When I come away bits are aching.' 'It is a workout.'

The facilitators recognized the value of music-making for their older participants' physical wellbeing, citing specific instances of improved health. Singing in particular was perceived as having a direct benefit for physical health through lung use and oxygenation of the blood. The physical nature of some music activities encouraged the use of warm-up exercises by facilitators, such as stretching and controlled breathing. Examples of participants' and facilitators' perceptions of physical benefits are given in Box 4.1. Some commented on the benefits to posture and fine motor coordination (see Box

4.2). Also reported were a range of non-specific health benefits. Examples of these are set out in Box 4.3.

BOX 4.1 IMPACT ON LUNG FUNCTIONS

Always feel better after singing. My asthma has almost disappeared.

The singing helps in my control of breathing.

Since becoming a member of the Sage Silver Singers (2004) my lung capacity and singing voice have improved, in my opinion.

Singing in choirs has helped me relax and feel more healthy – those breathing exercises really *are* good for you!

It has improved my breathing and helps me to relax and feel less anxious.

When she says about 'breathe in, breathe out', it's the air to your lungs. That's a health benefit, isn't it? But apart from that and moving your arms and hands ... but apart from that it's a chair-based activity, isn't it? Other than moving about on your legs, it is chair-based. I certainly feel good when you breathe in and you breathe out, you feel the air get into your lungs.

There is a lady in the [choir]s who is in a wheelchair. She is a wheelchair user and she has various conditions and one of them is connected with her breathing. And she started coming to the [choir] about three years ago, three-and-a-half years ago maybe and she has always had an operation every year to help her with her breathing and then when she started singing she didn't need to have this operation that year because her breathing improved substantially. And that's, you know, a very physiological thing.

I think physically there is a logic. I mean, there is clearly something different; the physical thing of singing and the actual health benefits of the physical singing, of the physical playing of pans – that sort of thing. It's not just

---

the physical, you know, the oxygenation of their good sing. It's how you feel after you sing.

I will give you an example. When I first joined I couldn't walk up those stairs. You know the stairs that go down to the rehearsal rooms. Walking up I was like this [demonstrates heavy breathing] and that was four years ago. Now, I don't have a problem. My lungs have definitely improved. Definitely improved!

Music for Life Project participants

Box 4.2 Benefits to movement and posture

And your body, because you are getting up and down all the time and then using all of your body to sing. If you are using it correctly and standing in the correct way, your hands are in position, your head's up and so is your chest and so forth, so all of your body is involved in it and your brain is certainly involved in it.

Playing the ukulele is good exercise for my finger joints.

Music for Life Project participants

Box 4.3 General health benefits

I think if you are happy doing what you are doing that's a health benefit in itself.

I was in a meeting last week where I was talking to people and there are a lot of people in the programme for whom this has had enormous benefits. People who would talk about health issues they'd had and how this has been their one thing, you know. So, there are certainly a lot of people in the programme for whom it has been a very important thing for their wellbeing.

> I think it is good for me. If it's good for me and I do it, it is good for me. That's my rule of thumb, you know. .... I feel much better when I do things ... much, much better.

> A lot of them actually do tell you. They say 'Oh, you know, we feel much younger'. Or if they have an illness, they say 'I am getting better and I think the music has a lot to do with after it'. So, you do get a lot of feedback like that.

> Everybody turns up perhaps even if they are not feeling quite so well. And you do feel better and you find it beneficial even if you haven't been ill.

> Since I started again after having a long break I felt an awful lot better taking the activities again.

> Music for Life Project participants

While the participants may not have mentioned the benefits to physical health as frequently as those relating to psychological wellbeing, during the focus group discussions it was suggested that musical activities should be available on prescription from the National Health Service and that making musical activities widely available could have a cost benefit for the health service.

> I would like to see 'singing as prescription' being offered by GPs. Newcastle has 'exercise as prescription' – singing could be offered, too, maybe with a friend to link the referred person.

> I think as regards funding it must save the health service and the social services an enormous amount if they put these in place everywhere ... it must be good for our health to get us out of the house so that we have to walk about and all the things that we are supposed to do.

> Participants, Music for Life Project, Ukulele group

Music and health: the future

There is increasing recognition that music can play a part in promoting and maintaining good health. Models of how this might operate are being developed. For instance, Bonde (2011) sets out a descriptive theoretical model of what he calls 'health musicking', which is reminiscent of the idea of the 'therapeutic choir' (Zanini and Leao, 2006), discussed in Chapter 2.

Bonde defines 'health musicking' as the common core of any use of music experiences to regulate emotional or relational states or to promote wellbeing be it therapeutic or not, professionally assisted or self-made. He proposes that 'health musicking' is related to four major purposes or goals:

- the development of communities and values through musicking
- the shaping and sharing of musical environments
- the professional use of musicking and sounding to help individuals
- the formation and development of identity through musicking.

Related to this is the concept of 'community music therapy'. This is similar to community music in that the musician accompanies participants and promotes community singing. It differs from community music in that the community music therapist has the needs and potentials of participants with health problems as the focus. 'Community music therapy' is viewed as a means of improving health and promoting human development (Stige, 2010). It offers opportunities for marginalized individuals or communities to thrive and develop. It creates a cultural and social link between music therapy and music and health in everyday life (see Trondalen and Bonde, 2012 for a review). Currently, there are no commonly established procedures or techniques in community music therapy. The therapist therefore needs to adapt activities to specific settings and contexts. Going forward, one such context might be providing musical activities for older people with the purpose of maintaining their physical health and wellbeing.

Summary

Music's impact on psychological wellbeing and subsequently good health is largely, although not exclusively, through the emotions it evokes. The specific ways in which the emotions are invoked depends on complex interactions between the nature of the music, the individual and the context. Music has a particular role in the reduction of stress and anxiety and, related to this, the reduction of pain and the strengthening of the immune system. Music can also support lung function, speech impairment, mobility issues, and motor coordination. Some research has reported general health benefits. Some of the Music for Life participants and their facilitators reported physical health benefits of music participation. These physical benefits included those relating to respiration, exercising, and increased movement. Singing was perceived as having a direct benefit for physical health through oxygenation of the blood and lung use. Thus, there is increasing recognition that music can have health benefits. New approaches to the role of music in health promotion include the concept of 'health musicking' (Bonde, 2011) and 'community music therapy', which differs from community music in that the prime focus is the needs and potential of participants with health problems. These approaches provide a framework where the strong links between music-making, health promotion and active ageing may be explored, with potential powerful positive benefits for participants in the Third and Fourth Ages.

Section Two

Musical development and
quality in facilitation,
teaching, and learning

2

Chapter 5

Musical development during the Third and Fourth Ages

This chapter focuses on the potential for older people to develop a musical self-concept, acquiring musical skills and understanding throughout the Third and Fourth Ages. We argue that personally meaningful musical development is entirely possible throughout the latter stages of life. Individual stories drawn from the Music for Life Project demonstrate that some participants considered themselves to have become 'musicians'. For some, participation in music brought a sense of continuity to their lives, providing a vehicle for connecting with the past. For many, opportunities to perform as musicians played an important part in this process. The extent to which a musical self-concept may contribute to subjective wellbeing and active ageing is considered.

The capacity for musical development during the Third and Fourth Ages

Few would dispute the claims that older people can and do continue to learn and develop in a number of ways, across the Third and Fourth Ages (see Chapter 6). The idea that opportunities for progression pathways in *music* should be available to lifelong learners of all ages is enshrined in the United Nations Seoul Agenda for Development of Arts Education (UNESCO, 2010). Yet, the idea of musical learning and development in the latter stages of our lives has received little attention in music education practice and research.

Musical development, encompassing skills, knowledge, and creative musicianship, has largely been regarded as being the dominion of younger people (Myers, 1995). Indeed, music education research has been called predominantly 'child-centric' (Dabback and Smith, 2012: 231), lagging behind other disciplines with regard to attention to older adult learners. Some studies in the area of musical participation and ageing have noted increased skill and enhanced musical self-concept amongst participants, but rarely has this been the focus of the research. Thus, while research has demonstrated the potential for *children* to develop skills in five distinct areas of musical performance, including sight-reading, performing rehearsed music, playing from memory, playing by ear, and improvising (McPherson, 1995/6), the question of whether older adults can develop in these areas, and what support they need in order to do so, has not been investigated extensively.

Although there is some evidence that there may be, in early childhood, 'a possible sensitive period for musical training' (Penhune, 2011: 1126), this does not preclude the idea that musical development may continue throughout our lives. Indeed, it has been claimed that all humans have a musical reserve capacity – an underused part of fundamental human musicality – that can be activated and developed at any stage in the lifecourse (Gembris, 2012).

> I get a feeling of doing something better each week and definitely feel I am learning and improving while enjoying myself.
>
> Ingrid, aged 76, Music for Life Project

What is musical development?

There is a long history of research concerned with the development of musical ability, or musicality. In much of the literature these terms are used interchangeably. Musicality has been theorized in several different ways. Many musical development studies have been concerned with measurement of progress in capacities to 'abstract, name, measure, and hold musical elements constant (e.g., pitch, duration, interval) across changing contexts' (Bamberger, 2006: 71). While early research in the area of musical development relied heavily on psychometric testing and was underpinned by the idea that musicality was innate, more recently 'musicality' and 'musical ability' have come to be understood as being influenced by personal (e.g. motivation, musical self-concept) and socio-cultural factors (Hallam, 2006a; Hargreaves and North, 1997). For example, a series of studies that explored understandings of 'musical ability' (reviewed in Hallam, 2006a) revealed different conceptualizations of this term amongst musicians, non-musicians, adults, and children, although the strongest agreement was 'in relation to rhythmic ability, organization of sound, communication, motivation, personal characteristics, integration of a range of complex skills, and performing in a group' (Hallam 2006a: 101).

Tests of musical aptitude amongst older people

An early study that investigated older people's aptitude for music was carried out by Gibbons (1982). Specifically, she was interested in the ability to notice differences in musical phrases. One hundred and nineteen independently living older adults aged 65–93 took part, completing the Musical Aptitude Profile (Gordon, 1965). Participants were required to listen to musical examples, marking on a sheet of paper whether pairs of musical extracts were the same or different, or whether the answer was not known. The test included three groups of extracts that differed with regard to tonal imagery, rhythm imagery, and musical sensitivity. Gibbons compared the scores of participants aged 65–70 (n=38) with their peers aged 71–75 (n=43), and 76–93 (n=68), finding little evidence of any differences between the groups. Although the study was limited by a predominantly female sample and a lack of ethnic or socio-economic diversity amongst the participants, the results suggested that 'music ability does not significantly decrease with age' (Gibbons, 1982: 28).

Another noteworthy early study that investigated the capacity for musical achievement amongst older people was carried out by Myers (1988). A programme of sequential musical instruction was offered to groups of adults representing early adulthood (aged 22–37), middle adulthood (aged 50–59) and older adults (aged 60–76). A total of 32 novice musicians, of whom 18 were in the older adult group, took part in at least 16 hours of instruction. The programme focused on developing aural discrimination skills, using movement, singing, and instrumental playing (recorder, autoharp, and guitar). Musical skills of all of the participants were tested before and after the programme of instruction. All of the age groups increased in skill and there was no evidence to suggest that increasing age should be a disadvantage for musical development. Indeed, in this study the older adults performed better than their youngest peers in the melodic reading-singing tasks.

Since those pioneering studies, the argument that older people deserve high quality musical opportunities has been advanced (Dabback and Smith, 2012; Gembris, 2008; Gibbons, 1985; Prickett, 2003), with growing evidence that lifelong learning in the creative arts, throughout the Third and Fourth Ages, is entirely possible when programmes are structured appropriately (see Chapter 6).

Constraints on musical development in Third and Fourth Ages

The arguments in support of the idea of lifelong learning in music do not diminish the real constraints – the 'gritty realities' – that some older people face (Formosa, 2011: 327). For example, Gibbons (1983a; Clair, 1996) followed up her earlier studies with some research that demonstrated difficulty amongst some older people with noticing small interval changes or changes in pitch duration, and imitating of complex rhythms. Some of these difficulties were explained by short-term memory lapses. A further challenge faced by many older people is some extent of hearing loss, which is associated with a reduced pitch range (Greenwald and Salzburg, 1979). Prickett (2003: 62) notes that 'the pitch ranges and keys we often use with children to encourage singing with a head voice are uncomfortably high for older singers'. Old age may also bring reductions in reaction time and attentional resources (Cohen, 2009).

Gembris (2008: 103) summarizes some of these challenges, noting that an 'important aspect of making music in old age is the limits and possibilities of musical performance in this stage of life. Due to age-correlated constraints, they are to be expected in cognitive, sensory and motor areas.' However, Gembris does not interpret these constraints as an argument against the possibility for musical development in older age. Rather, he applies the concept of 'selection – optimization – compensation' (Baltes and Baltes, 1990) to explain how older adults may mitigate some of the challenges of ageing, in their music-making.

A study carried out by Gembris (2008) demonstrated that older learners in music were selective about the pieces they played (selection), were focused in terms of their use of practice time (optimization), and had developed a range of compensatory strategies in coping with the physical and technical demands of making music. Responses from 308 senior members (average age 71) of community orchestras in Germany, Switzerland, and Austria indicated that half of these older amateur orchestral players experienced some kind of physical (e.g. respiratory problems, restricted mobility), slowing down (e.g. finger mobility, reaction time), cognitive issues (e.g. short-term memory), and sensory constraints (e.g. vision and hearing). Nonetheless, self-perceptions of musical performance standard were high; more than 50 per cent felt that they were reaching between 80 and 100 per cent of their best performance, and nearly 20 per cent thought that they had attained their best musical performance between the ages of 60 and 69.

The participants identified a number of coping strategies that helped to mitigate some of the physical, cognitive, and sensory challenges noted above. The strategies could be grouped as physical (e.g. doing special exercises, playing sitting down, using special visual or hearing aids), mental (e.g. acceptance and accommodation, patience, humour, calmness), and musical (e.g. shorter, more efficient practice sessions, selecting in which pieces and activities to take part, reducing the musical demands, playing from notation instead of by memory). A similar typology of compensatory strategies was noted by Bruhn (2002), amongst older amateur and professional musicians in Germany, while Dabback (2005: 7) stated that 'older adults usually compensate without extreme intervention and without drastic impact on achievement'.

The concept of crystallized and fluid intelligence may help to understand the process by which older adults engage in selection (Box 5.1), optimization, and compensation (Box 5.2) to lessen constraints that are related to ageing. Crystallized intelligence, concerned with wisdom, life experience and cultural knowledge, has been found to increase with age. This contrasts with fluid intelligence, concerned with problem solving that is independent of experience, which is said to decline with age (Stuart-Hamilton, 2006). It may be that an increased reliance on crystallized intelligence can account for some of the compensatory strategies that older adults apply in their music-making (Cohen, 2009). The distinction between crystallized and fluid intelligence is in accordance with a view of ageing that recognizes that older adulthood may be a period of change where, alongside some potential decline in certain capacities, older people may 'consciously draw on their accumulated experience in developing new concepts' (Myers, 1995: 22).

The principles of selection, optimization, and compensation were illustrated by singers and instrumentalists in the Music for Life Project. These older people spoke about their decisions to invest precious time in activities that were meaningful (Box 5.1). Others described a range of strategies that compensated for some age-related challenges (Box 5.2).

BOX 5.1 SELECTIVE INVESTMENT OF TIME IN MUSIC-MAKING

Eric recalls that his parents enjoyed singing: 'Father was a bass, mother was a very high'. His granddaughter plays the guitar and he enjoys sharing folk music with her: 'she's given me a new lease of life'. He has never participated in a musical group before and does not participate in any other leisure activities apart from his singing group, which he has attended for five years. Now aged 77, Eric is limited in his activities by Parkinson's disease.

> I'm enjoying it ... it's not a waste of time. Something rubs off on us. I don't [do other activities], no I don't unfortunately. Look I have Parkinson's. It's curtailed me, tremendously ... so it's [singing] opened a whole new world to me ... I like the people, I feel we're not wasting our time ... We all feel it's not a waste of time, it's good for all. I think music has benefits for everybody, if they bother to listen, or even taking part, or singing.
>
> Eric, aged 77, Music for Life Project

Box 5.2 Compensation strategies

Guitar and ukulele players in the Music for Life Project took part in a focus group interview, describing the various challenges they faced in learning their instruments, and strategies they applied in order to meet these challenges.

> I came with a very good right hand; with the ability to pluck the strings but my left hand for the chords was weak ... so I have come back to the intermediate group where I have to practise moving my left hand with the chords, which is what I need the practice on ... Because I am retired I do a lot of practising.

> I haven't played any music for 47 years so coming back was difficult. ... So I had to set myself a slot every day to make myself practise.

> The thing is that you can always fake it, you know ... [Group laughing] You can play the easy chords.

> You can play the first chord and the ones you know and you add volume to them which are the important ones. It doesn't make any difference whatsoever to the ensemble. It's that you are part of the group and you should be there. Because you are supporting the group and you can sing with what you know and you play the chords you can. Next year it will be twice as many [chords].

> I am not good at reading tablatures and I can't even begin to start to do it; I understand the concept of it but I need a lot more practice so I am just happy to leave it out and just strum away.

> I make time. I really do make time. I try to practise every day if I can because it's the only way.

> Music for Life Project participants, Guitar and ukulele groups

Of course, it must be acknowledged that some older people face significant challenges that have a profound impact upon quality of life. Such challenges may, for example, include the experience of stroke, Parkinson's, or dementia (see Chapter 3). For these older people, there is some evidence that music-making helps to retain skills and to develop new skills. For example, Vella-Burrows (2012: 8) states that 'people living with dementia can learn new musical material', citing a case-study example of people with dementia who had, with support, written and performed their own song-cycles. Likewise, Morrison and Clift (2012b: 10) provide the example of a singing group for older people with mental-health issues, where the facilitator reported 'great moments of musical breakthroughs'. Indeed, creative arts sessions for older people in residential care have been shown to play a vital part in holistic care, with individuals creating, sharing and being challenged within structured, stimulating arts activities involving music, movement, and reminiscence (Fraser, 2006; 2009). Thus, particular care should be given to inclusive, imaginative practice that ensures that frailty does not become an insurmountable obstacle to accessing high-quality opportunities for musical engagement and development.

The need for progression pathways

Like anyone of any other age, older people need and desire progression pathways. Meaningful participation in musical learning involves activities that embrace 'principles of lifelong learning and vital engagement', with sequential progression pathways and proximal challenges (i.e. challenges that are attainable, with appropriate support) (Dabback and Smith, 2012: 231). Chapter 6 provides an account of the ways in which progression in music amongst older people may be facilitated.

The view that older people want to progress and develop as musicians has been supported by a number of pieces of research. For example, Gibbons (1982) reported, of the 152 independently living older people she surveyed, 84 per cent indicated that they wanted to improve their current musical skills. In a similar vein, Darrough and Boswell (1992) described the commitment to musical progression amongst older adults in the Phoenix area of the USA. Each year, the older population in this area increased during the winter months, with an influx of 'snowbirds' – retired people taking advantage of the warm local climate. Instrumental and vocal groups were offered through the local community; choral groups of all description performed in local festivals. When asked whether they regarded their music-making as musical, social, recreational, or therapeutic, the large majority of older people in Darrough's choir responded that it was first and foremost a 'musical' experience, placing emphasis on the desire to achieve meaningful musical results in performance.

Musical progression routes have been found also to be a priority amongst adult piano students. Jutras (2006) surveyed 711 adults (average

age 51 years) who learnt the piano, 55 per cent of whom learnt in groups. The age range of respondents was 24–94, with 72 per cent over the age of 40. Participants wanted to improve their piano technique, musicianship, musical and theoretical knowledge, and listening skills. Overall, acquisition and refinement of musical skills were rated as the most important reason for participation – more important than personal (e.g. stress reduction, fun, self-esteem) or social-cultural benefits (e.g. cultural understanding, new friends, sense of belonging).

Participants in the Music for Life Project reinforced the view that progression was a priority in their music-making (Box 5.3). Marcia, recently retired and a novice music-maker, spoke of the thrill of achieving the 'right' sound, and how important it was to her to be able to improve in this regard. Patrick, who had been an amateur musician throughout his adult life, spoke of the challenges relating to mixed ability groups, supporting the idea that groups should be organized in such a way as to allow for progression.

Box 5.3 The need for progression pathways

I think I can do better than I am, and that's why I came here ... there are moments when we get the right kind of sound out with an amazing bit of harmony – I think, I can't believe we've done it ... the performance we did at the public library, we liked it that they asked for us back again. I don't think that we were that good but we turned up and we did our best ... I just want to do better, it's something that's very important to me. Just talking to you about it has put it into my mind what I want, I want to get better and I don't want to go term after term just to do a bit of community singing.

Marcia, aged 72, Music for Life Project

I am up for the challenge! I need a challenge ... I wouldn't want to be involved in something that has far too many beginners, real beginners. I mean, it's nice to try and help beginners but I think you need to have segregation of ability to some extent, because it can become very frustrating for the better players who are wanting to play music to have a constantly disrupted and spoiled [rehearsal] from people who are not up to it. So, I do think you need to segregate

> ability to some extent ... We have different levels and
> people move up as they gain experience. They move up to
> the next group up.
>
> Patrick, aged 67, Music for Life Project

Evidence of musical development in the Third and Fourth Ages

An Australian rock-band project provides a case-study example supporting the view that ageing need not be detrimental to creative musical activity. The 'Weekend Warriors' targets older people who are described as 'dormant' musicians – individuals who wish to keep alive memories of past music-making, or who have a vision of becoming involved in music-making during retirement (O'Shea, 2012: 199). O'Shea (2012) carried out a study of one Weekend Warriors six-week project, with activities that included a jam session, coaching sessions, and a charity gig where each band contributed a half-hour set. O'Shea was interested in the goals and the learning pathways of two rock bands. The Third Age musicians (aged 46–64, with a median age of 57) were observed in their music-making and were interviewed during the project and again several weeks later. All of the musicians had musical family backgrounds, although the skills and aspirations that they brought with them to the project differed considerably. While some wanted to 'play good rock music', 'take on a new musical genre', and 'learn confidence and skills', others wanted to 'make musical contacts' and 'become a rock diva' (O'Shea, 2012: 212). O'Shea noted considerable achievements amongst the musicians, with regard to learning, performing and progressing. In some respects, their maturity helped them to work collaboratively (going on to form their own band – the Hot Vox), whilst acknowledging individual differences in musical preference, ability, and personality within the group.

Similarly, progression in musicianship and collaborative learning was noted amongst a group of older adult piano learners. Pike (2011) carried out a mixed-method longitudinal study following the progress of a MIDI piano ensemble comprising 35 participants aged 65–95. Participants worked towards individual goals within a context where the emphasis was on collaboration, peer learning, and celebrating achievements with outreach performance opportunities. In addition to a number of social-emotional benefits, Pike noted a marked improvement in musical quality and ensemble cohesiveness, with progression being promoted by peer support and modelling.

A survey of 62 directors of New Horizons Bands and Orchestras (catering for senior citizens) across the USA and Canada was carried out by Cohen (2009), exploring perceptions of how older learners engaged with the programmes. The directors were asked to compare their older learners with younger groups. While some directors reported that older people were more resistant to change and slower at grasping new ideas, others reported that the older adults actually learnt faster, being better at remembering analogies, better able to respond to requests for expressive playing, and demonstrating a more nuanced understanding of the music than their younger counterparts. Cohen (2009) suggests that these different responses may relate to the types of tasks that the directors had in mind when responding. While some may have been referring to tasks that required fluid intelligence (which, as noted above, is thought to decline with age), others may have been focusing on tasks where crystallized intelligence was an asset, requiring a depth of understanding that had been acquired through life experience.

Musical self-concept and its relationship with musical development

For people of any age, a strong musical self-concept is linked with musical development. Motivation and goals in music are linked with the extent to which individuals perceive themselves to have a positive possible self as a musician (Hallam, 2006b). Many studies have suggested that through music-making, older people discover or rediscover a musical self-concept that is underpinned by new skills, increased confidence, and creative activity (Creech *et al.*, 2013c). Through participation in musical ensembles, the identity of 'musician' is conferred upon individuals. This may be reinforced and affirmed through interactions within the musical group and beyond, from family and friends (Dabback and Smith, 2012).

Research has demonstrated the potential for participation in music to function as a medium for expressing one's inner self, defining oneself, and providing a sense of continuity in one's life. For example, interviews with 38 seniors aged 60–98, exploring the meaning of music in their lives, revealed that 'music provides a way for people to explore who they are and express themselves to others' (Hays and Minichiello, 2005: 274).

Similarly, musical identity was a prominent theme amongst eight keyboard learners aged over 60, who learnt as a group in a workshop setting (Taylor and Hallam, 2008). Some of the keyboard players had reframed past perceptions of themselves as unmusical, experiencing 'a fresh start with the discovery of unexpected skills and talents' (Taylor and Hallam, 2008: 301). For others, their current music-making was seen as a means of reconnecting with youth and of feeling empowered. For all, a musical identity was linked to feelings of satisfaction with life. The keyboard players gained confidence from playing together in a supportive workshop setting, where individuals felt it was safe to make mistakes.

The possibilities for developing a new musical self-concept, as well as for revising or reclaiming a lost musical identity, were articulated by members of a New Horizons Band in the USA. The New Horizons Bands function as an entry to instrumental music-making amongst seniors, catering for all levels, including complete beginners. Dabback (2008b) carried out several focus groups with members of the band. Some included 'newcomers' who had been participating for less than five years, while others included 'old-timers' who had been playing in the band for five or more years. In some cases, band members had developed musical self-concepts that were in direct contrast to earlier self-perceptions as non-musicians. In others, individuals with some musical experience now experimented with new facets of music-making. For example, women chose to learn instruments such as tuba, drums, and saxophone 'that were once off-limits' because of their male-gendered associations (Dabback, 2008b: 278). Musical identities amongst the band members were reinforced by new skills, roles within the ensemble, and affirmations from the wider community, outside of the ensemble.

Possible selves

The idea of 'possible selves' (Markus and Nurius, 1986) refers to future-oriented selves that are domain specific, guiding action and influencing decisions regarding in what to invest effort and what to abandon (Smith and Freund, 2002). Possible selves are also dynamic, in the sense that individuals may reframe their possible selves in response to life transitions, motivated by the desire to preserve wellbeing (Cross and Markus, 1991).

Possible selves amongst older people have been explored. One study investigated whether the older people's possible selves would focus on desires for self-improvement or, alternatively, would be concerned with efforts to prevent losses. During face-to-face interviews with a sample of 206 people aged 70–103 drawn from the Berlin Ageing Study, the participants were asked to describe their hoped-for and feared possible selves. Across all ages of participants, the dominant motivational orientation for hoped-for selves was the desire to attain, achieve or re-experience something, while for feared possible selves the dominant orientation was avoidance. The recorded possible selves were found to be highly personalized, dynamic and varied, covering a range of domains, even amongst the oldest old (Smith and Freund, 2002). When the interviews were repeated four years later, 72 per cent of new possible selves were related to hopes, compared with 53 per cent that were related to fears. This research supported the view that late adulthood need not be interpreted as a period of disengagement from planning for new possibilities and experimenting with new possible selves.

Frazier *et al.* (2002) suggest that future-oriented images of self amongst older people are underpinned by identity-relevant goals. Their research focused on the hoped-for and feared possible selves reported from 151 residents of senior residential communities in Florida, aged 60 to 96. Overall, leisure, health, and enhanced abilities/education were found to be the most important hoped-for possible selves. When age differences were examined it was found that while abilities/education were the most important domain for possible selves amongst those in their 60s and 70s, health was the most important domain for those aged over 80. The researchers concluded that through pursuing goals associated with possible selves, individuals continued to construct their own development through the latter stages of life.

For possible selves to support positive wellbeing, they must be salient, in the sense that they are both psychologically accessible and personally meaningful (Rossiter, 2007). This salience is strengthened when possible selves are constructed through the observation of role models, experimentation with provisional selves and evaluation of new conceptions against internal and external standards (Ibarra, 1999). The more vivid the possible selves become, the more they motivate individuals to strive towards narrowing the gap between the current self and the possible self.

King and Hicks (2007) emphasized the importance of salience and elaboration in their discussion of how adaptive possible selves may influence adult development. By 'salience' they referred to the extent to which the possible self is available and the individual is engaged with the associated goals. The concept of 'elaboration' refers to the richness of the narrative individuals can generate when asked about their possible selves, including the vividness, detail and emotionality. Individuals with well-elaborated possible selves are not only better able to face failures but they also have access to more strategies to avoid failure (Leondari *et al.*, 1998).

Possible musical selves

For many older people who participated in the Music for Life Project, music was a vehicle for redefining one's identity or rediscovering a lost 'possible self' (Creech *et al.*, 2013c). It was striking that many participants formed future-oriented images of their selves that were framed by the idea that 'I am a musician'. For some this involved drawing upon past experience, while others experimented with a new musical identity.

Musical self-concept was bolstered by a sense of being part of a community of musicians and by having performed alongside their professional musician facilitators. Participants also referred to how they thought others perceived them; being a 'musician' was a new, purposeful role, bringing with it interest and importance (Box 5.4).

BOX 5.4 BECOMING A MUSICIAN IN THE THIRD AGE

Singers and instrumentalists in the Music for Life Project took part in focus-group interviews, where they spoke about their musical possible selves.

> It has made a big difference to my life. After retiring at 59, I now (65 now) consider that I have become a musician. I write songs, I perform and I play guitar.

> Relatives, friends, some of them are quite intrigued. Particularly when you mention the [performing arts centre] they think you are a wonderful singer.

> You stop counting your rhythm you feel it in your blood.

> Do you see yourself as a musician? – Yes, I do.

> I think if I was doing that on my own I wouldn't feel like a musician but when I hear the sound of everybody playing together, I do.

> In the beginning I was very embarrassed about singing and anybody hearing me sing. So I always chose a good singer next to me so that she would carry me along, you see. But now, no, I am not embarrassed any more. I feel my voice has developed.

> The guitar is always in the ring now. It's always around the house. I will pick it up and play.

> I used to watch instrument groups like that and I thought 'I could never do that. How do they know what to do?' But now we know all the signals. It's like a secret code really and we know how it's done now and we feel ... I feel so clever doing this.

> Music for Life Project participants

For many participants performances offered an important opportunity to 'be a musician', sharing the results of their hard work with friends and relatives. Performances were opportunities for positive feedback and contributed significantly to a strong musical self-concept and social affirmation. A minority indicated that they did not feel comfortable about performing, attributing this to a lack of confidence. Others did not enjoy performances when they perceived their contribution to be a limited, token gesture. On the whole, performances that were valued and meaningful were interpreted as a significant part of the participants' individual and collective musical journeys (Box 5.5).

BOX 5.5 THE BUZZ FROM PERFORMANCE

Aisha (aged 72) lives alone in sheltered housing. She has little musical background and had lacked confidence in joining the group. She says she had never sung, before joining the choir.

> When we perform we know that we watch the tutors and they expect a lot from us and we want to give it because we have such a good rapport with them. And I mean the audience is always so appreciative. Oh, wherever we go. It's lovely getting that buzz and you really do your best. You feel really good after because you are on a high, you know. Yeah, really nice ... We gave a concert just before Christmas and the audience were amazed. My daughter was there and she couldn't believe it. Because they encouraged us, you know, to dress like rock in leathers and other stuff and you should see the pictures ... I am seventy-two, you know and we are all at that age and you should see the way we come from the start. Very nice [laughing].
>
> Aisha, aged 72, Music for Life Project

Musical possible selves and subjective wellbeing

As discussed in Chapter 2, engagement in musical activities has significant potential for supporting subjective wellbeing, conceptualized as comprising three underlying constructs: purpose, autonomy/control and social affirmation. This chapter has illustrated how highly valued possible musical selves can provide a sense of individual and shared purpose in the lives of many older people. Music-making provides structure in daily and weekly routines and can function as a medium through which seniors pursue goals and acquire new skills. Alongside the Music for Life Project, other studies (e.g. Dabback, 2008b) have reported examples of older people deriving a renewed sense of purpose from their possible musical selves, placing a high value on their music-making and developing a detailed understanding of the steps that need to be undertaken in order to develop as musicians.

Possible musical selves have also been found to be related to a sustained sense of autonomy and control in individuals' lives. For example, some participants in the Music for Life Project spoke of having the freedom, in later life, to explore these possible musical selves. Others spoke of how 'being a musician' provided the opportunity for self-expression and individual creativity. Being a 'musician' was linked with growing confidence, contributing one's own ideas, and taking some control in musical contexts (Box 5.6).

BOX 5.6 AUTONOMY AND CONTROL IN POSSIBLE MUSICAL SELVES
Singers and instrumentalists in the Music for Life Project took part in focus groups. Denzel described how his experience in the electric guitar group had spurred him on to take control of his own learning. Albert and Patrick noted the importance of being able to contribute their own ideas during rehearsals, highlighting how important it was to them that their facilitators respected their views and were responsive to their input.

> Funny thing that happened – we've got a guy who left us now … and he would sort of watch and say 'How do you do that?' It's difficult to explain how you play by ear. But I have answered one time and I said 'Go home, get that Guitar Hero, plug your guitar and push yourself forward'. And I, myself, went home after that and thought 'Bloody hypocrite you are. You haven't pushed yourself forward!' So it has given me a kick off the back side, you know, to take control.
>
> Denzel, aged 81, Music for Life Project, Electric guitar group

> If it's something that doesn't suit us, or we are not happy about, we say 'Oh, don't you not think such and such?'… occasionally we'd say 'Do you not think that perhaps this might be better if we did it this way?' And the tutor would turn on say 'Well, yes, good idea! We are doing that then' …

> it's not pupil and master sort of level. You know, we are all at a level.
>
> With the group here we do have a leader. She is not a teacher, she is a leader. And we all contribute. Some are more expert than others, to say the least, so we all input ideas.
>
> Albert, aged 80, Music for Life Project, Choir member

Musical performances have been found to offer an important context where older people receive social affirmation and validation as a 'musician'. In the Music for Life Project, provided that performances were perceived as being valued and meaningful, rather than limited token gestures, they functioned as a significant part of the participants' possible musical selves (see Box 5.5, above). As musicians, individuals could contribute to their communities and provide pleasure and enjoyment for others. In turn, these individuals experienced a strong sense of affirmation as a valued member contributor within their immediate social context (Box 5.7).

BOX 5.7 SOCIAL AFFIRMATION FOR POSSIBLE MUSICAL SELVES
Members of a ukulele group discussed their experiences of performing for others. Mona (aged 77), Nahla (aged 73), Nadir (aged 78), and Olga (aged 80) had all started learning the ukulele after age 70.

Mona: Well, another thing is that we play at old people's homes. It has been really nice to share with them and we've got a good response from them. They had a good time and they asked us back and it's nice to give things.

Nahla: I used to take my ukulele into the care home where my mum was – and the staff used to love it. And I used to stand behind her because I knew I am not a very good player, self-conscious, but it was really good.

Nadir: I think we need to have something to aim for otherwise we might just waft along and not bother. So it makes all the difference if people are going to be dedicated. Well and if it's a free show, that's nice. I'd rather give a free show. I don't want to be paid for anything.

Olga: I mean, we went three weeks ago to give a performance and we were very well received. We had a wonderful afternoon and it's that sort of thing that is very satisfying. Well, we just want to give something back.

We don't want payment or anything. I think it's nice just to go round. That was wonderful, wasn't it?

All: It was a brilliant afternoon!

Music for Life Project participants

Summary: musical progression and active ageing

Does progression within the framework of a musical possible self contribute to active ageing, in later life? The evidence presented in this chapter suggests that older people who became actively engaged in music-making formulated future-oriented identities that provided a sense of purpose in later life, some extent of sustained autonomy and control, and a strong sense of social affirmation. Through the context of music-making, individuals could freely experiment with provisional musical selves, which in turn provided structure, a framework for new skills, enhanced confidence, the scope for creative expression, and the scope for making valued contributions to the wider community. As such, for these participants, progression in music and the development of a musical identity supported subjective wellbeing and played a vital role in sustaining active ageing.

Chapter 6

Principles and practices of facilitating musical activities for older people

This chapter explores the principles and processes involved in facilitating musical activities for older people. Perceptions of the role of the facilitator as well as issues relating to inclusive practice, curriculum, goals, and progression are identified. Strategies for enhancing teaching and learning in musical groups are highlighted. The chapter includes examples from facilitators' and participants' accounts of their experiences. These examples are framed by background literature concerned with the principles and practices of 'geragogy'. The chapter puts a strong focus on challenging the myth that older people cannot or will not learn new knowledge and skills, emphasizing the qualities and practices of facilitators who provide effective support for maximizing the wider benefits of engagement with music, and fostering musical development amongst groups of older people.

Introduction

Within the wider field of education and training, little attention has been paid to the principles and practices of facilitating learning amongst adults in the Third and Fourth Ages (Formosa, 2002). In music this omission is particularly salient (Gembris, 2008; Prickett, 2003; Tsugawa, 2008). Relatively little previous research has been directly concerned with the learning and teaching processes that underpin the positive outcomes that were discussed in Section 1 of this book.

The relative lack of interest in issues relating to facilitating music with older people is evidenced in the UK by limited Continuing Professional Development opportunities for facilitators of programmes for older people (see Creech *et al.*, 2012 for a list of relevant organizations). For example, the UK government guide for routes into teaching music (Rogers, 2005), aimed at 'every kind of musician', makes no mention of the specialist skills and knowledge that may be required for working with groups of older people. However, some lessons may be learnt by examining the wider field of learning and teaching for older adults.

Why do older adults engage in learning?

Lifelong learning has been linked with active ageing (WHO, 2002), and is advocated as a means for empowering individuals, supporting independence, developing skills and competency, and contributing to sustained personal fulfilment and wellbeing (Dench and Regan, 2000; Glendenning and Battersby, 1990; Withnall, 2010). As noted in Chapter 3, continued engagement in learning has been found to be one significant route through which mental capital (cognitive, social, and emotional resources) amongst older people may be preserved (GOScience, 2008).

It is not the case that any educational opportunity for older people is 'good' *per se* (Formosa, 2002). Rather, the value of engagement in learning during the Third and Fourth Ages is related to opportunities for self-directed and self-regulated learning, collaborative dialogue and reflection, and for real and sustained development of knowledge, skills, and wisdom. These ideas formed a cornerstone of the framework for critical educational geragogy (CEG), whereby teaching and learning for older people is seen as a context for transformation, emancipation, and empowerment (Formosa, 2002; 2011).

While there are several theoretical interpretations of the value of later life learning (Withnall, 2010), it is clear that older people themselves are a heterogeneous group with diverse and complex orientations to learning, expectations, social and individual capital as well as constraints. Whether the purpose of education for older people is focused on the wider benefits to be derived from active participation in learning or alternatively on the moral imperative to provide equal access to transformative and empowering learning for all, it is important that facilitators of older learners are equipped to respond to a range of motivating factors amongst participants across the Third and Fourth Ages. In particular, an inclusive definition of active ageing requires that learning opportunities celebrate and are responsive to the participation of all, including the oldest old (Walker, 2008). From the perspective of CEG (Formosa, 2002) it is the voices of older learners themselves that provide the most salient lessons as to how learning during latter life stages may most effectively be supported, so that the promises of transformation, empowerment, and enhanced wellbeing and mental capital might be realized.

Implications for facilitators of musical activities for older learners

When one considers the powerful arguments in favour of learning in later life, together with the growing body of compelling evidence that demonstrates the potential for music to support social, emotional, physical, and cognitive wellbeing, it is clear that the issue of how to maximize the benefits of musical opportunities for older people is critical. Access to opportunities for engagement in later-life learning and participation in music is not, on its own, enough to ensure that the potential benefits noted above are optimal. Practitioners must be able to recognize and respond to myths about older learners as well as responding to the real barriers that act as constraints in later life learning.

By definition, any attempt to draw up a list of recommendations for facilitating groups of older people in music runs the risk of disregarding the learner voice, subscribing to the myth that all older learners are the same (Findsen, 2005), and reinforcing a view of active ageing that potentially excludes those in the Fourth Age. Indeed, Withnall and Percy (1994) caution that any prescriptive statements about older learners risk underestimating the rich diversity to be found amongst our older population. However, research concerned with later-life learning outlines some broad areas where enhanced knowledge, skills, and strategies may support facilitators in developing musical activities that foster the positive benefits of music and learning that have been described above.

Myths about later-life learning

Findsen (2005) identified three pervasive myths about older learners. The first relates to the idea that older people comprise a homogeneous group, with a collective set of needs. This view is clearly not sustainable. Indeed, it is arguable that as people accumulate life experience they become ever more diverse (Audit Commission, 2008). As Seltzer and Yahirun (2013) point out, labels such as 'elderly' and 'senior' mask the diversity in life histories that is shaped by gender, education, work history, socio-economic status and a host of other factors. Withnall (2010), who carried out extensive focus-groups with a total of 98 older learners in formal educational settings, referred to 'the diversity of the older population and the sheer difficulties of disentangling the relative effects of different influences on individuals at different times'. Any attempt to characterize older learners as a homogeneous group thus risks being 'misguided and ageist' (Withnall, 2010: 118–19).

A second myth is the idea that all older people are characterized by decrepitude and diminishing capability. There is evidence that fluid intelligence, associated with processing speed and short-term memory, does decline as humans age. However, crystallized intelligence, acquired through experience and reflection and associated with knowledge and wisdom, has been found to remain stable or even increase. To conceptualize learning as being associated solely with fluid intelligence risks underestimating the potential for older adults to develop mental capital. Furthermore, there is evidence that amongst groups of older people the individual differences in these measures of crystallized and fluid intelligence become greater, meaning that while some people experience decline others increase (Glendenning, 2000). With sufficient opportunity for practice, motivation and time, learners in a number of domains have been found to achieve equivalent outcomes to their younger peers (Charness, 1992). In music there is evidence that older learners develop compensatory strategies to mitigate physical or cognitive constraints (Coffman and Levy, 1997; Gembris, 2008). Furthermore, later life has been depicted as a period of profound creativity, where older people use creative outlets for reflection on their own unique stories and for personal healing and problem solving (Hickson and Housley, 1997).

The third myth highlighted by Findsen (2002) was that of dependence, with the related positioning of older learners as consumers. Rather than dependence, the Third and even Fourth Ages may be conceptualized as periods of interdependence, where an intergenerational exchange of knowledge and skills becomes salient, and where older learners comprise a rich resource for knowledge and skills. For example, Flowers and Murphy (2001: 32), who interviewed 45 adult music learners aged 70+ about participation in musical activities, reported that 'older adults can serve as resources ... in their broad perspective about the function of music throughout life and its implications for music goals and curricula ...' The drive to engage in purposeful and meaningful activity, together with the need to make a socially valued contribution, persist through the Third and Fourth Ages (Weiss and Bass, 2002). From this view, older people have the potential to continue in a relationship of interdependence within their families and wider communities.

The myths outlined by Findsen (2002) provide a useful framework for facilitators to reflect upon their own underlying assumptions about older learners and to develop their practice with positive and creative approaches. For example, facilitators can be guided in developing strategies for differentiation, responding to the diverse needs of heterogeneous groups. Active ageing may be supported through tasks that capitalize on crystallized intelligence and the capacity for dialogue, reflection, and creativity. Approaches that embrace the prior experience of participants, encourage older adults to recognize and develop compensatory strategies, and that foster interdependent learning, may also support sustained engagement with learning.

The role of the facilitator

Research concerned with teaching older learners in a variety of domains (Duay and Bryan, 2008; Hickson and Housley, 1997; Villar *et al.*, 2010) suggests that the interpersonal qualities, teaching strategies, skills, and knowledge of group leaders may be particularly important in mitigating age-related changes and challenges. Facilitator qualities that have been identified as contributing to positive outcomes for participants include enthusiasm, respect for participants, clarity and organization, interest in participants' prior knowledge, credible subject knowledge, and responsiveness to diverse needs within a group. Effective facilitators have been found to employ a range of strategies to spark interest and sustain motivation (Duay and Bryan, 2008). These include the use of humour, clear visual and aural stimuli, and stress-free activities that avoid timed tasks (Coffman and Levy, 1997; Southcott, 2009). The 36 older learners in Duay and Bryan's qualitative study highlighted the value of an open style of questioning, time for discussion and social interactions, and time for practising new skills.

Withnall and Percy (1994) suggest that the role of facilitators is to discover what participants wish to achieve and to consider how to provide an enabling physical and psychosocial environment that meets these goals. An enabling environment needs to be one where participants have the means to take responsibility for their learning, bring their own insights, and contribute to developing individual and collaborative goals. Barriers to participation for older learners can be psychosocial factors such as fear of failure, reluctance to engage with unfamiliar tasks, and perceptions of procedures as being very complex (Withnall, 2010). Thus, it is crucial that an atmosphere of respect and trust is established, characterized by 'listening, love and tolerance' (Formosa, 2011: 327).

Research concerned with leadership styles in teaching offers some insight with regard to the implications of a range of facilitator approaches. Several frameworks for facilitator style have been proposed (for example, Heron, 1999; Jones, 2005). Amongst these, three broad facilitator orientations have been identified: hierarchical and authoritative, democratic and co-operative, and collaborative and focused on supporting learner autonomy.

Within the first hierarchical approach, the leader transmits or delivers content to the learner. The leader is the gatekeeper (Jones, 2005) to the material being learnt, while the participant's role is to absorb this material and then be able to reproduce it. Although participation in music involves practical skills and active engagement, research has shown that surprisingly often ensemble leaders adopt a hierarchical approach, dictating the curriculum, selecting repertoire and making decisions as to how it will be played, technically and musically. Music sessions led by 'gatekeepers' tend to be dominated by teacher talk or modelling interspersed with learner performance, with little variety. Essentially, the participants play and the facilitator talks or models the desired performance (Creech, 2012; Creech *et al.*, 2013d).

With specific reference to facilitator styles that enable learning amongst older people, a more dynamic use of all three orientations may be most effective. Within the democratic approach, for example, the responsive leader acts as a facilitator who aims to enable participants to discover the content and processes for themselves. Although this is to some extent learner-centred, the leader selects the material and constructs activities in order to maximize positive learning outcomes. This style of leader typically makes extensive use of 'scaffolding' (Creech *et al.*, 2013d), whereby participants are supported in appropriate ways to achieve challenging yet attainable goals. Thus, this approach requires the leader to take into account the needs and capacities of the participants when choosing or creating the material and activities.

The collaborative approach may be described as learner-centred, with the support of autonomous, self-directed learning as a core principle. In this approach, facilitators and participants focus their energies on discovering new material together. Egalitarian relationships are encouraged. Participants may thus feel more able to contribute their own ideas and sometimes will take on leadership roles within the group. The group may become a learning community, characterized by collective exploration. The life experience and insights that all adult participants bring to the group are acknowledged and valued.

In the following sections of this chapter some key messages from research concerned with facilitating older learners in transformative and empowering learning and teaching contexts will be explored and linked with the voices of participants and facilitators who participated in the Music for Life Project.

Making use of prior knowledge

A consistent message relating to supporting older learners is concerned with recognition of prior knowledge and life experience (Withnall, 2010). New knowledge and skills need to be assimilated into existing cognitive structures and understandings of the world; learning will therefore be most effective when new ideas are connected to and build upon prior knowledge and real life experiences. Meaningful material reduces the demands on working memory, captures the interest of participants, and helps to sustain motivation. In music, use of material that is well known and meaningful in relation to participants' autobiographical experiences will help to make explicit the relevance of new skills and activities and will serve as a 'common ground' from where facilitators might expand the repertoire (Box 6.1).

> ### BOX 6.1 JACK'S STORY – MUSIC AND MEMORIES
>
> Jack (age 85) described himself as having had a 'beautiful voice' as a young boy, recalling having loved music and singing in particular. Jack's young adult life had been defined by service in the Royal Navy. Throughout his story, Jack emphasized the meaningfulness of music from his early adult years.
>
>> Any dance music. I love a lot of the old songs, there's feeling in them, I mean, [sounds upset] this particular tune to me is very emotional to my late wife as well and that's a very old number which goes 'Tonight, I mustn't think of her, no more memories tonight, tonight I must forget how much I need her, so Mr Leader play your little tune ... etc. [sings – word perfect] The old numbers that had a meaning to them ... I love the, the other two old chaps who sing the Irish songs, it's lovely, it's lovely music. The music today the younger generation lap up, it doesn't appeal to me. The song that I've just sung to you and music in those days, it was music, it meant something. The words meant something ... I'm 85, it gives me a great feeling inside me that I can sing and it makes other people happy ... I think it's the music. It seems that people I've never met in my life, we're closer, we're much closer together now than when I first met them.
>>
>> Jack, aged 85, Music for Life Project

In musical contexts, skilful choice of repertoire is one obvious means by which prior life experience of participants may be recognized and celebrated. Explicit links between repertoire and participants' life experience underpinned the most successful groups participating in the Music for Life Project (Box 6.2).

> ### BOX 6.2 RICHARD'S STORY – MUSICAL CHOICES AND LIFE EXPERIENCE
>
> Richard (age 86) recalls starting to sing at school, around the age of 10. He remembers liking it when his teacher played the piano and sang, describing her 'croaky' voice. Early on, around age 11, he learnt

the violin at school and he describes a specific memory of performing 'Drink to Me Only with Thine Eyes' for his class. Another strong memory is of going with a group of ten children to sing in a large children's concert at Crystal Palace, where he and just two others were given a 'third' part to sing, in the midst of many hundreds of children. Richard has very strong associations between singing and camping. As a young lad a formative experience was his membership of the 'Woodcraft Folk' (a youth movement devoted to teaching the skills of living close to nature, first set up in 1924 in South London) where he learnt many campfire songs that remain his favourites now.

> I've done it all me life. From the age of 10 at least ... The teacher, when she played the piano, I liked it when she played the piano and we sang. I tried to learn the violin. So I played this violin, 'Drink to Me Only with Thine Eyes', I could just about manage that. I went to Crystal Palace, do you know of Crystal Palace? They used to have a children's concert there, and a number of us from the school, about 10 of us ... we were singing third part, you can imagine this bloody great round, in a half circle, massive, and there must have been a thousand kids, something like that, and there was three of us singing third part! That was it, three of us singing at Crystal Palace, third part, the rest just drowned us out. So we did our best, whether we were any good or not I don't know. My voice wasn't that well developed. But I was always in that sense interested. And one of the things I did with my singing see, I was a king camper, so I sang round campfires. So I was singing round campfires very early in my life. Because I was in the Woodcraft Folk, so what songs was I interested in? The ones you sing round campfires [sings a campfire round] ... Now, if there was a choir going every day, I'd be there every day. And I think a lot of it is social, it's not just the singing. I think singing has been a social arm for me because I like people ... (The songs we do) – they're popular, you know what I mean, they go back in time. So they're easy to sing if you listen to them. So I like him (the facilitator) in that way. ... of course the thing that I can sing for him and it's the only

> thing I can remember the words to is 'Drink to Me Only with Thine Eyes'.
>
> Richard, aged 86, Music for Life Project

Generally, facilitators in the Music for Life Project agreed that older people liked to engage with familiar music that related to their life histories. Notwithstanding this, there were examples of successful engagement with unfamiliar and challenging material and a subsequent sense of achievement for participants. At times facilitators had to make difficult judgements relating to how much to challenge participants as opposed to offering more familiar activities and repertoire. Although the benefit of going beyond what the participants felt comfortable with was recognized, it was also advocated that building a trusting relationship with the group was important before introducing challenging material (Box 6.3).

BOX 6.3 FACILITATORS' PERSPECTIVES – LINKING REPERTOIRE TO PRIOR EXPERIENCE

It's essential that repertoire is appropriate to the group; it's always helpful if we're doing songs that the group recognize or relate to. That said, it's also good to challenge them, provided it's balanced with enough familiar/easily accessible repertoire ... I think there has to be that element of pushing people to do a bit more than what they expect they can do because then the satisfaction that people get from that is much greater ... We sing a lot of Gershwin, jazz, eclectic songs but I've tried to do a sort of range. And when we have done music from other cultures it works pretty well I think. I know some members of the group have really liked it when we've done some African songs ... We did a Japanese song in Japanese last spring, so singing in different languages. There's a little bit of inertia and I have to go over that but I think once it's done, then it's like wow we sang that Japanese song! ... I've known most of the group for a few years now, I feel I can try things and they will come with me now whereas in those very early days to try some African music or singing in a different language or music from a very different place to what they

> were used to sometimes didn't work ... A good session is ... if we get to the end of the class and I feel it's been a nice variety, but it's been stimulating, I've got a response and some unexpected responses ... We did the Abba [song] for the first week and I just thought it was quite interesting to see Hilda, 92, singing Abba and really, really involved.
>
> Facilitators, Music for Life Project, community music choirs and singing groups

Active learning

There is strong support for the view that effective learning will take place when knowledge is actively constructed, rather than transmitted. A survey of 2645 adults aged 50–74 revealed that Third Age adults perceived their learning to be most effective when tasks were self-paced and framed within a longer training period than a traditional structured lecture (Boulton-Lewis, 2010). A constructivist approach to working with older learners has been advocated, whereby 'teaching older learners is most effectively accomplished by actively encouraging and inviting their participation and input, thereby capitalizing on their collective prior knowledge and life experiences' (Spigner-Littles and Anderson, 1999: 204).

This constructivist approach (Spigner-Littles and Anderson, 1999: 206) can be initially challenging to older learners who may be 'emotionally attached to the beliefs, knowledge, values, and world views that they have developed over a period of many years'. Some older learners may initially seek directive teaching from their facilitators, as this may strongly align with their prior experiences.

Box 6.4 introduces Edith, whose story suggests that she is most deeply engaged with music when she is *making* music, and that she values authoritative, as opposed to laissez-faire, leadership that supports the attainment of high standards in her music-making.

Box 6.4 Edith's story – the case for authoritative leadership

Edith (aged 80) remembers singing with her sister as a child and describes music as a lifelong pleasure. She stopped music-making when she married but promised herself she'd take it up again when she retired. She is now part of a singing group that has gone into local schools and shared their wartime experiences with the children, through music. Music, for Edith, is most meaningful when she is actively participating, singing. Edith's musical taste is eclectic ('anything except rock and roll') and she belongs to four very different choirs, focusing on diverse musical genres. She emphasizes that a good facilitator is an expert who takes learning and performance seriously and supports the choir in achieving their performance goals.

> If you start with say 5, 6, 7, me and my sister used to go to bed not with bedtime stories but with the National Song Book, and we used to sing the ones we knew, we'd learned at school, we used to sing those till we went to sleep, if we didn't know what the tune was we made one up ... And I promised myself when I was 60 I would restart learning the piano because I wouldn't be able to sing any more, but because I can still sing I haven't started to play the piano! ... The trouble with going to concerts is I want to join in! I mean it's fine if it's a work I don't know because I've got to listen to it but if it's something I know [hums].
>
> What makes a good leader of music? Someone who knows what they're talking about. Someone who's fairly strict in fact and doesn't stand for any nonsense ... you get people who want to chat. ... a choir is there to get on with the job and get it as good as, and get it to performance standard. If I'm going to perform I want to do it right.
>
> Edith, aged 80, Music for Life Project

Autonomy support

In keeping with principles relating to wellbeing and active ageing, engagement in learning amongst older adults may be most powerful when the context is one where participants may exercise their own judgement and take control of their own learning (Spigner-Littles and Anderson, 1999; Withnall, 2010). This may include having an input into setting goals and planning the location and timing of activities as well as the content. There is clearly a place for flexibility and negotiation on the part of facilitators in meeting this need. Facilitators can support older learners in developing new skills, but more crucially can also help their participants to develop self-regulation strategies.

In music this may require creative and innovative approaches that might include incorporating group review of their music-making, collaborative goal-setting, developing non-linear activities that accommodate learners who drop in and out, and developing practice strategies that compensate for some age-related constraints (Gembris, 2008). Participants in the Music for Life Project corroborated this view (Boxes 6.5 and 6.6).

BOX 6.5 PATRICK'S STORY – ENCOURAGING HIGH EXPECTATIONS

Patrick (aged 67) claims that as a child he never took advantage of opportunities to learn instruments. It was only as an adult, while working abroad, that he became interested in Early Music and took up the recorder. Now aged 67, he values leadership qualities that include the ability to guide and enthuse participants, to offer expertise and set high standards yet also to encourage and value input from group members.

> They [good facilitators] know how to go about instructing and guiding people in a tactful way. So I would list knowledge, first of all, enthusiasm, but then, the right sort of personality to be tactful and nice to people and helpful. Encouraging people. One person that I think is incredibly good – he is an exceptionally good musician but he has this ability to get the best out of people. He pushes quite hard actually but in a very nice way. He doesn't make you feel hopeless, demoralized, but he pushes quite hard. Expects the best from you. And it is quite a subtle difference between somebody who expects the best and demoralizes everybody because they can't keep up.
>
> Patrick, aged 67, Music for Life Project

BOX 6.6 JULIA'S STORY – AUTONOMY SUPPORT

Julia (aged 79) and her husband are members of a local choir. Music has been an important part of their adult lives together.

> It's not pupil and master sort of level. You know, we are all at a level ... He doesn't make it too formal. He does make amusing remarks and the sort of exercises we do at the beginning, which you didn't see many of today, but some of

> them are really funny, you know ... I think in many cases,
> the tuition is tailored to the level of talent and ability that
> is within the group that he has. ... he responds and works
> in that level. ... The first thing he has to have, obviously, is
> a sense of humour. And he has to, and he certainly does,
> realize that while he is there he is one of us. He is not the
> Master 'I am teaching you'. Because I have said some of
> them are probably teaching him ... Must know the subject,
> obviously, and the ability to convey the knowledge that he
> has. Not to pitch it too high ... He doesn't turn up and say
> 'Oh, you can't do that. You must be like that.' So flexibility.
> He must be taught to be very flexible.
>
> Julia, aged 79, Music for Life Project

Interdependence

A predominant message from the wider literature concerned with teaching
and learning suggests that peer interaction offers a powerful vehicle for
learning (Wood *et al.*, 2010).

Amongst older learners peer learning has formed the cornerstone of
many educational contexts (Clark *et al.*, 1997), offering opportunities for
mutual moral support, sharing knowledge and developing ideas.

In musical contexts, a small amount of literature has focused on
the idea of interdependent peer learning amongst young musicians. These
few studies support the view that peer relationships developed within the
context of music-making serve an important motivational function and are
strongly associated with continued interest and involvement in music (Creech
and Long, 2012; Kamin *et al.*, 2007; Patrick *et al.*, 1999). The concept of
interdependence is salient for older learners in music, too. For participants in
the Music for Life Project, making music in a group was a powerful context
for learning new skills, experiencing a sense of purpose and achievement and
forming social networks (Box 6.7).

> BOX 6.7 BRIDGET'S STORY – INTERDEPENDENCE IN A MUSICAL
> GROUP
> Bridget (age 63) had no formal education in music and says that
> she never sang, 'not even in the shower'. She grew up in the north
> of England, amidst the post-war burgeoning rock and pop culture.

After early retirement from a career in the civil service she joined a community choir as a way to mix with other people and because she believed it would help her to maintain a sense of wellbeing.

> You meet a lot of other people from all backgrounds and experiences and knowledge ... One of the things that intrigues me about it is how a group of people who have never met before, hardly know each other, can quite – and it will happen tomorrow – I'll probably know about quarter of the people there tomorrow – would in four hours produce this piece of work, which you know, makes people outstanding. So, it's that stimulation. People are committed to things, getting on with it. And you are always learning something which I find, to me, through the music programme, it is one of the more important things. I think it is the meeting of other people with like minds and the social interactions but also singing ... I think you feel support from everybody. If there is a concert, we are all together in it and you feel everybody is there for you.
>
> Bridget, aged 63, Music for Life Project

Creativity

Notwithstanding some iconic examples of creative achievements in later life, creativity is not the preserve of the 'great and gifted', nor is it limited to young people. Rather, creativity is 'an attribute of every individual' (Hickson and Housley, 1997: 41). Reflections on life experiences, for older people, may bring a renewed orientation towards creative endeavours.

The idea of lifelong growth in creativity has been supported by research evidence. For example, 55 older adults participating in a Quality of Life Programme demonstrated increases in creativity measures (Goff, 1992), while 36 older (aged 60–93) contributors to an art exhibition attributed a sense of competence, purpose, and personal growth to their participation in creative activities (Fisher and Specht, 1999). The key implication for facilitators is that older people continue as creative individuals through the Third and Fourth Ages and engagement in expressive, creative activities can in turn support healthy ageing. Box 6.8 demonstrates how one facilitator of a weekly singing group aimed to develop creative activities in her sessions, including improvisation and composition.

> **Box 6.8 A facilitator's perspective – creative music-making**
>
> We are also trying to get more creative now because at the beginning we were quite repertoire based, which in some ways felt right because I think it took some … a bit of encouragement sometimes to get people to feel like they can do it (improvise) and it wasn't too scary … as the facilitator, first of all, [my aim is] to try and draw out basically the interest and enjoyment of music for the people who are involved in the group … bring in the musical ideas and the creative approaches, so as to be able to help people enjoy music and being creative … doing something creative and whatever it is about music. There is this magical thing about music that makes you feel good.
>
> Facilitator, Music for Life Project, Singing group

Creativity did not necessarily rely on composition or improvisation approaches. Music for Life Project participants described how the sheer act of making music had the potential for creative expression and interpretation. Box 6.9 illustrates how creativity could be experienced through expressive performance.

> **Box 6.9 Elizabeth's story – creativity in singing**
>
> Elizabeth (aged 76) has been involved in music for most of her life, playing the piano and singing in a range of different groups. She describes the scope for creative expression in choral singing.
>
> Everybody doesn't mind working hard because at the end when you've got everybody that knows what they are doing, it all comes together and you can enjoy the creation of what you've done. As I said that is part of being part of a choir. It's the creativity of it all, isn't it? Because no matter who is in it, it's gonna sound different to somebody else's choir. You know, it's those particular voices and feelings that are different in everybody else's choir and everybody's choir isn't the same, they are all different to one another.
>
> Elizabeth, aged 76, Music for Life Project

Meaningfulness

Meaningful activities are broadening and gratifying experiences where participants continue to feel that they matter to others (Weiss and Bass, 2002). As such, meaningful activities are related to the idea of social affirmation, discussed in the Introduction of this book. Meaning can be derived from activities where participants make an emotional investment and commitment. This personal investment in an activity can be supported when physical and social contexts are enabling and consistent. Continuity involves routine and physical comfort, but it also involves a consistent sense of being valued for the contribution made. Meaningfulness is also found when activities are clearly linked with goals and achievements.

In addition to the personal meaning derived from engagement with music that had strong links with personal memories and experience, participants in the Music for Life Project spoke about a sense of purpose and social affirmation achieved through their music-making. As previous research would suggest, these aspects of meaningfulness were most strongly supported when participants had musical goals and aspirations that were valued and respected.

In particular, facilitators noted that groups often thrived when they were offered performance opportunities. Performances were thought to provide important goals and to support participants' enjoyment of performing. The participants recollected significant moments and made reflective comments relating a sense of relaxation, achievement, collective effort, and the buzz that they had felt during performances. They also talked about how special it was for them to connect with the audience (Box 6.10).

> **BOX 6.10 CLARISSA'S STORY – THE MEANINGFULNESS IN MUSICAL PERFORMANCES**
>
> Clarissa (aged 77) has a musical background and is a member of several groups, including guitar, ukulele, and steel pans. She is a pianist with long experience of teaching piano and playing for amateur operatics. She now accompanies two singing groups and conducts one choir.
>
> > In performing, you are allowing people to hear you; you want to feel that what you've learnt is going to be enjoyed by someone else ... You feel that it's a nice ending to weeks and weeks of hard work, you know. You feel great! That's good. I feel satisfied now, you know. That you've done something

> and somebody else has appreciated it. And you feel 'Oh, yes we have accomplished something'.
>
> Clarissa, aged 77, Music for Life Project

Summary

Within a social context where the fastest growing age cohort is the over-85s, there is a burgeoning interest in the potential for learning to support active ageing. Some have recognized the potential for learning to be transformative and empowering for older adults, particularly when teaching and learning contexts privilege the voice of the older learner and involve collaboration, dialogue, self-directed activities, and reflection.

Although the wider field of educational gerontology has produced research that has clear implications for facilitators of groups of older learners in both formal and informal contexts, little, if any, research has been specifically focused on facilitators of musical activities. However, there are several key messages for musicians who work with older adults. First, the notion that older people are all the same and that they are decrepit and dependent consumers needs to be dispelled. Secondly, facilitators need to develop a wide repertoire of enabling strategies that meet the diverse needs of their participants. Finally, it is incumbent upon facilitators to support older people in their personal investment in activities that are creative and meaningful, where each individual makes a valued contribution and also progresses towards personal and collective goals.

Chapter 7

Active ageing through intergenerational music-making

This chapter reviews previous research concerned with the role of intergenerational music-making. We highlight ways in which intergenerational music-making may provide a rich context for the development of social relations and interactions between seniors and children or young adults, supporting the dimensions of wellbeing that include purpose, control/autonomy, and social affirmation. The idea of generativity, referring to the importance for older adults of 'making a lasting contribution' is applied in the discussion of how intergenerational practice may support subjective wellbeing during the Third and Fourth Ages.

Intergenerational practice: an introduction

There is no single definition for describing intergenerational practice. In the UK this term is used to refer to 'purposeful activities which are beneficial to both young people (normally 25 or under) and older people (usually aged over 50)' (Hatton-Yeo, 2006: 12). Although in the general literature the term describes 'a social phenomenon that brings together the oldest and youngest generations' (Newman *et al.*, 1997: 3), we need to acknowledge that groups of older people can in themselves be intergenerational, sometimes covering several decades (Frego, 1995; O'Neill and Heydon, 2013). An intergenerational dynamic is also fostered when the group's leaders are representative of the 'middle generation' (i.e. 25–50 years old), working alongside older people in creative and meaningful activities (Springate *et al.*, 2008).

The main purpose of intergenerational practice 'is to bring together different generations to collaborate on purposeful activities, while supporting and nurturing each other in meaningful ways' (Hermann *et al.*, 2006: 124). These interactions amongst different generations enable growth and provide 'the kind of purposeful existence that is important to human development' (Newman *et al.*, 1997: 19). Three types of intergenerational programmes where mutual support and nurturing could be fostered have been identified: activities in which older adults provide service to children or youth; those in which children or youth assist the elderly; and cooperative programmes where different generations collaborate on activities as equal partners.

> It's good to sing with the younger generation, and the older generation as well, mixed, we get experience from each other.
>
> Anne, aged 78, Music for Life Project

Intergenerational projects in the arts involve a variety of creative interactions, such as storytelling, arts and crafts, music, dance, and drama (Hatton-Yeo, 2006), which foster benefits including increased understanding, friendship, enjoyment, and confidence (Springate, *et al.*, 2008). Benefits specifically experienced by older people are linked to reduced isolation through social interaction (see Chapter 2) as well as a renewed sense of worth derived from the experience of contributing to the lives of younger people. This links to the concept of generativity (Erikson, 1963), discussed later in this chapter. Benefits reported by younger participants link with the development of self-esteem (Springate, *et al.*, 2008), interpersonal attachments and relationships, and the dissolution of stereotypes (Herrmann, *et al.*, 2006; Meshel and McGlynn, 2010).

An additional key benefit to intergenerational practice is its potential for enhancing lifelong learning and skill development amongst both the young and the seniors. The significance of learning in later life and its relationship with active ageing has been well-documented (Mehrotra, 2011; Schneider, 2011) and is discussed in Chapters 3 and 6. As this chapter illustrates, intergenerational music-making provides a rich context for lifelong learning.

Generativity in intergenerational practice

As we approach the latter stages of life, the urge to inform and guide the next generation becomes stronger (Erikson, 1963). This phenomenon is known as 'generativity', where older people pass along values, culture, and life skills to members of the succeeding generation in an endeavour to improve the world, offer service to others, and 'contribute something worthwhile to the betterment of society' (Herrmann, *et al.*, 2006: 135). In this vein, Anne, a Music for Life Project participant, spoke about why the intergenerational sessions were meaningful, explaining that 'Children are the community aren't they? They will be building our community for the future.' Erikson (1963: 267) advocated that 'the concept of generativity is meant to include such more popular synonyms as productivity and creativity, which, however, cannot replace it'. In the absence of generativity the individual feels a 'pervading sense of stagnation and personal impoverishment'.

Generativity may be evident in social, political, or cultural activities where older people contribute to the experience of younger generations (Rubinstein, 2002). A sense of meaningfulness derived from intergenerational activities fosters improvements in generativity. 'When meaning is absent or lacking, the beneficial aspects of programme participation seem to rapidly evaporate' and 'result in the erosion of psychological wellbeing' (Hermann *et al.*, 2006: 135).

Intergenerational practice could be seen as a particularly important facet of active ageing, providing people at all stages of the lifecourse with opportunities for preparing for, supporting, and modelling active ageing. Walker (2008: 87) recognized that 'opportunities to develop activities that span the generations' are important features of active aging. That is to say, the sense of generativity (to disseminate skills, facts, and ideas) expressed by the seniors creates a unique synergy with the sense of industry (to learn new skills, facts, and ideas) exhibited by children and young people.

Generativity, wellbeing and active ageing in intergenerational music-making

It has been observed that intergenerational practice enhances the creation of interpersonal attachments, promoting social involvement and engagement (Cusicanqui and Salmon, 2005; de Vries, 2012). Similarly, intergenerational music-making is a context where individuals may develop a sense of mutual concern, caring and respect for each other's musical preferences, abilities, and interests (Conway and Hodgman, 2008; Darrow *et al.*, 2001; de Vries, 2012). Intergenerational practice in musical contexts may support active ageing in a number of powerful ways.

First of all, musical activities may contribute to a developing sense of generativity amongst older participants, offering opportunities for leaving a 'legacy' through direct collaboration with younger generations. Closely linked with this is the idea that intergenerational practice in music can support three facets of wellbeing, identified as social affirmation, purpose, and control/autonomy (see Introduction). Generativity and subjective wellbeing are, arguably, closely related underlying dimensions of active ageing (Walker, 2008; World Health Organization, 2002). A positive relationship between generativity, singing, and wellbeing has been reported by O'Neill and Heydon (2013), who found that wellbeing was enhanced through shared intergenerational musical interactions. Within intergenerational activities, older people can engage in purposeful activities that 'make a difference' to their younger counterparts. The life experience, insight, and wisdom that older people bring to intergenerational groups can be a source for social affirmation. Within expertly facilitated groups, a sense of control and autonomy may also be supported through activities where the older people can contribute in creative and expressive ways.

Intergenerational musical practice can serve as a means of integrating diverse populations and people of diverse abilities, in collaborative activity (Darrow *et al.*, 2001). Music may function as a 'pathway for deepening intergenerational communication and understanding' (Conway and Hodgman, 2008: 325). Cusicanqui and Salmon (2005), for example, explored the benefits of an intergenerational singing group involving eight pupils (aged 10 and 11) from an elementary school, singing together with seniors living in a New York settlement-house residence. The programme's aim was to learn the basics of singing/voice and to build up a sense of community for the participants. The two groups did not rehearse together regularly but met three times to sing together. The final session was an informal performance to fellow senior residents. The concert was thoroughly appreciated by performers and audience alike, fostering a strong sense of purpose amongst the participants, whose hard work and musical achievements were acknowledged. Through this intergenerational activity the children 'had developed more positive social skills and they appeared more confident, more enthusiastic, and appreciative of older people'. The seniors described it 'as a renewing of life' (Cusicanqui and Salmon, 2005: 207).

Other studies have shown that children's enthusiasm, interest, and ability to learn about music is enhanced during intergenerational programmes, whilst seniors feel worthwhile and productive through sharing knowledge and life experience (Frego, 1995; Garber, 2004; West, 2003). West (2003) and Garber (2004) explored how the songs of Tin Pan Alley were used as social, musical, and educational resources in music-making between children (aged 6 –11) and groups of elderly, disabled, and/or disadvantaged in the community. The children in the programme engaged individually with nursing-home residents through singing, movement, conversation, and physical contact, aiming to encourage participation amongst the seniors. Although the programme had a largely non-musical goal (the main focus was to make the nursing-home residents more physically active, improve their mental acuity and their emotional state through music) the children's enthusiasm for music was enhanced, as was their interest and ability to learn about music. Furthermore, performance anxiety was reduced. The older people benefitted from the interaction socially and emotionally in the sense that they felt that they could make a contribution to the children's development, through their responses.

Meaningfulness and an underlying sense of purpose are contributing factors to the success of intergenerational music programmes (Herrmann *et al.*, 2006; Newman *et al.*, 1997; Springate *et al.*, 2008; West, 2003). The repertoire selections and types of activities that both children or young people and seniors find enjoyable and meaningful could reinforce their sense of purpose for attending intergenerational music programmes (Conway and Hodgman, 2008; de Vries, 2012). Conway and Hodgman (2008: 227) found that the music itself, which in this case was Fauré's *Requiem*, appeared to be 'the most important positive part of the [intergenerational] experience' for the participants.

A phenomenographic, intergenerational study of three older Australians making music with children demonstrated how a sense of generativity amongst the older people was supported when they were encouraged to make meaningful contributions to the children's musical engagement (de Vries, 2012). The participants in the study were Irene (aged 67 years) and her granddaughter Chelsea (aged 11 years) who played piano together; Margaret (aged 75 years) who accompanied a school choir as a volunteer and taught Kylie (aged 8 years), one of the students in the choir, to play the violin; and Bruce (aged 72 years) who, together with his friend's son Josh (aged 15 years), played saxophone in his 1950s style rock and roll band. This study illustrated the significance of reciprocity of learning between generations and the great sense, amongst the older people, of being valued and respected by the children and others connected to the children, such as their school principal). The seniors described how the children had taught them how to use technology (iPod, Finale Notepad, and ProTools software programs), had motivated them to engage with music, and had also helped them to become familiar with contemporary repertoire. There was a recognition amongst the older people that their contribution to the children's musical learning had been significant – Irene expanded Chelsea's piano repertoire by introducing duets that they could play together, Kylie wouldn't have had the opportunity to learn to play the violin if Margaret had not volunteered to teach her, while Bruce supported Josh's development of technique on the saxophone, through regular rehearsals and performances with the band.

Amongst the greatest benefits of intergenerational practice is its contribution towards the dissolution of stereotypes, thus promoting a sense of intergenerational social affirmation. On the one hand, through their involvement children and/or young people dispel an image of ageing, often imposed by the media (Frego, 1995), as 'being over the hill, out of date, out of touch, frail, sick and in need of services and support' (Kerschner and Pegues, 1998: 2). On the other hand, seniors observe young people in creative and productive activities and develop positive attitudes about them dispelling perceptions towards children and young people as being 'rude' (de Vries, 2012: 346), or insensitive and inconsiderate (Darrow *et al.*, 2001: 45). The attitudes of intergenerational audience members towards teens and older people were explored by Darrow *et al.* (1994). Audience members of all ages completed attitude rating scales before and after an hour-long live performance of an established intergenerational choir. Overall, attitudes toward teens and seniors moved in a positive direction from pre-test to post-test. These findings signify that intergenerational musical performances may play an important role in modelling intergenerational affirmation and purposeful collaboration, bringing about change in attitudes amongst audience members as well as performers.

Intergenerational practice in the Music for Life Project

The intergenerational programme of the Music for Life Project, used here to illustrate the link between intergenerational musical practice and active ageing, provided an opportunity for older people and children to collaborate in music as equal partners. Creative music sessions with two groups of seniors started in October 2009. The sessions included singing, songwriting, and experimentation with untuned percussion instruments (Varvarigou *et al.*, 2013). From March until May 2010 the seniors were joined weekly by two groups of children from local primary schools for an intergenerational music programme. Three music facilitators with great experience in working with young people in the community led the creative sessions as well as the intergenerational programme. The programme culminated in a concert at the Pit Theatre, the Barbican Centre, London in May 2010.

Generativity

The Music for Life Project supported a sense of generativity in a number of ways. First, the older people played a central role in a musical performance for their families, community members, and for the younger people. The performance itself gave the seniors the opportunity to contribute to making a rich experience for the younger people, and to a most moving performance for the audience. Secondly, providing the children with experiences that could help them to think about how they themselves might age actively was another potentially significant and long-term benefit from intergenerational music-making. In this way, the project helped to break down stereotypes associated with ageing.

The idea of generativity may help to explain the motivation amongst the older people, who shared songs of their generation with the children of the intergenerational programme as well as contributing their own life experiences in creating new songs (Box 7.1).

Box 7.1 Benefits for the older people

Lately we've been having school children in here and we've been singing songs to them, and we've given them a song sheet with all the old numbers on them, and there was one group that came here, more juniors that sort, and they joined up as if they knew all the songs, they were in tune with us, it was marvellous, it was really lovely.

Older participants, Music for Life Project

From the children's perspective, intergenerational music-making encouraged a sense of musical security as the children felt supported by the seniors in group singing and collaborative instrumental playing (Box 7.2).

Box 7.2 Benefits to the children

I was hoping that the children were going to appreciate and enjoy working out at the [sheltered housing] and meeting the people there. I was also hoping that it would make them sing with a purpose ... I think being able to work together with a different group of people especially with the concert being the end product, it gives them a sense that music can be fun and can make things more alive and, I don't know, bring people together.

The whole participation, the whole collaboration with the singing and also playing instruments and just the whole interaction I think ... was probably the highlight for them. Going there [sheltered housing], singing with them, singing to them and then with them and the instruments and everything.

Teacher participants, Music for Life Project

I liked one thing about older people; that they really helped us and they played music and instruments very well.
I liked we were playing the instruments and when we are singing there is a tune behind us by old people.

Children participants, Music for Life Project

Autonomy/Control

It has been noted that intergenerational practice should be participative and empowering, with the younger and older participants learning together as equal partners (Springate *et al.*, 2008; Walker, 2008). To some extent, this was achieved in the Music for Life Project, where older people and the children were given opportunities to work together, with each group making specific contributions. For example, the children were invited to choose the actions to accompany each musical phrase of 'El Café', a traditional song from Argentina. This process helped all to remember the lyrics. Likewise, the seniors were encouraged to devise an instrumental accompaniment for the song using untuned percussion and to teach this to the children, who then joined with their maracas. Notwithstanding opportunities to add actions or a simple accompaniment to songs, supporting a sense of autonomy and control amongst the older people was one area of practice that proved to be challenging for facilitators. There was potential for a greater focus on activities that would promote reflection on their own experiences and hand ownership to the older people. For example, the older people's prior experiences could have been much more central in the musical activities with the children. Although the seniors did compose their own songs there was no input from the children during this process and it is suggested here that the children might have been even more engaged and interested in the older people had there been more intergenerational peer collaboration in the songwriting tasks.

Some of the challenges in maximizing the potential benefits to be derived from intergenerational practice related to the particular training needs of facilitators who work with older people (Box 7.3). Whilst the Music for Life Project facilitators were highly skilled and experienced in their work with young people, this project revealed some particular pedagogical issues relating to effective practice when working with older people (see Chapter 6 for a full discussion of these issues).

BOX 7.3 CHALLENGES IN INTERGENERATIONAL PRACTICE

Inclusion

> [Some seniors] are quite controlling of other people who are just frailer and sort of want to say what they can do when they can very easily speak for themselves.

Working with younger children - a lot of it is about getting them physical and active and a lot of warming up and you expect them to be able to do that, but here ... I think you have to think more carefully about it if you want to do physical warm-ups, for example, and always provide a kind of get out for people, saying 'don't do this if it doesn't feel right' or 'you can do this instead'.

Facilitators, Music for Life Project

Credibility

It's far more challenging than people realize to work with a group of older people particularly if you, yourself, are not that old. I mean, if you walk into a room looking like everybody's grandson or granddaughter you are stuffed really. And a lot of trainees and apprentices who work on the Youth side, predominantly maybe, ... they have a well-developed and successful attitude of how to work with young people - it's very different to work with older people.

Facilitators, Music for Life Project

Purpose

In accordance with previous studies, where it has been noted that preparing for a performance gives a specific purpose to intergenerational musical interactions (Conway and Hodgman, 2008; Cusicanqui and Salmon, 2005; Darrow *et al.*, 2001; 1994), the Music for Life Project intergenerational activities culminated with a performance at the Barbican Arts Centre in London – a high-status performing arts centre – where it could be seen that the programme was being taken seriously and was valued within a wider community. A rewarding outcome of the project was the 'heightened performance experience' (Conway and Hodgman, 2008: 227), which lasted for weeks (Box 7.4).

BOX 7.4 THE REWARDS OF PERFORMANCE

We were looking forward to doing the show and playing an instrument because I haven't got a tune in my head and

> I was on a high every Thursday and after the show it took me a week to calm down.
>
> Well, it [music-making] helps me. It makes me young. Without music ... I wouldn't be here [Barbican centre] ... Instead of sitting, watching TV, doing nothing. Look, we are here ... It was fantastic ... and I feel so young to be honest with you. And I am happy.
>
> It was outstanding and they [the facilitators and children] were wonderful and we blended in.
>
> As soon as we warmed up and we started singing, I had this lovely feeling of heart being in harmony. I mean, it was hard work. It was a big commitment ... but it was worth every minute of it really.
>
> Older participants, Music for Life Project

Social affirmation

Findings from intergenerational music programmes talk extensively about the positive impact of the interactive experience on social relationships, which often create feelings of belonging, enjoyment, and appreciation (Cusicanqui and Salmon, 2005; Garber, 2004; Varvarigou, Creech *et al.*, 2012b; West, 2003). In an example (Box 7.5), seniors, children, teachers, and facilitators intermingled around a circle. This enabled the facilitators to scaffold learning (Duke, 2000), by giving some initial directions and then letting the group interact and collaborate in warm-up music games or in developing musical/rhythmic accompaniments to the songs.

> ### Box 7.5 Collaboration during a music game
>
> Facilitators, children, and seniors sit around in a circle; the seniors on chairs and the children on the floor. They are playing the game 'pass the clap' as part of their warm-up, where a clap that starts from the facilitator is passed around the circle as fast as possible. In the first attempt the clap takes six seconds until it returns to the facilitator. The seniors look very eager to pass the clap as fast as possible. One of the seniors in the circle is blind and she does her best

not to delay her clap. The facilitator says 'This is going to be the world record. We need to get it down to at least five-and-a-half seconds'. 'Yea!!!' the group shouts. A sense of camaraderie has already developed among the children and the seniors, as they need to work together to achieve the 'world record'. Samir rolls up his sleeves in preparation for the second round. The facilitator says 'Like Samir, put your sleeves up' and the children do it immediately whilst Samir demonstrates how to do it. The eyes are on Samir now who rubs his hands together; the children and facilitators copy. They are getting ready for the second attempt. The class teacher is timing how long the second clap will take to move around. The eyes are on the facilitator now who gives the starting clap. The clap goes around very fast; both children and seniors look very focused. 'Five seconds', the teacher said at the end. Everybody cheers and applauds. 'That was amazing. I don't think we are ever gonna beat that' said the facilitator and a big smile appeared on everybody's face.

Music for Life Project participant

As reported in the studies noted above, the children in the Music for Life Project found the seniors to be funny, kind, and loving (Box 7.6). The teachers emphasized that the children bonded with the seniors and developed respect for them. The teachers also recognized that music functioned as a vehicle for enhancing mutual understanding amongst the generations.

Box 7.6 Social affirmation through intergenerational music-making

The best thing about singing and playing music is that the experience was great with the old people.

It was good because better than singing with young people it's just that you can express yourself.

It was very fun singing and playing instruments with the older people. It was fun going there.

And when we were at [the sheltered housing scheme]; these were the most fun days of my life with Anne and Samir and the rest of the crew.

I was very happy. It was very fun to sing with older people because older people could sing with us.

I loved it and hope I will go again and I liked making the old people smile.

Children participants, Music for Life Project

I think just seeing how the children kind of bonded and respected and were fond of the people at [the sheltered housing]. We really grew fond of them, you know, Rick and then you've got Anne and Hugh with his phone going off all the time. We just became almost friends with them. I didn't expect that. I was worried that ... not sure about working with old people but they were so lovely! And of course Samir. How can I forget Samir? So, we'd love to go back and keep up the link.

For them [the children] working with older people [was the best part of the programme] because not all of them have got grandparents, or the very young children – their grandparents are not as old as some of the people that are there. And then we had children, Year 3, a young lad in Year 3 and he loved talking to old people. When he was there chattering away about all sorts and he actually was one that couldn't get to go to the Barbican for lots of reasons ... He was the one child that they all asked about – all the old people. And they came and said 'He was so full of life'. So that was coming from them. I was getting feedback from them and they thoroughly enjoyed it – their [the children's] enthusiasm and being so full of life.

It was something different, something that they hadn't done before – working with the elderly. And they did all thoroughly enjoy it. They were a little bit worried at first but once they got there they really enjoyed it. And they were looking forward to going back again and again. You know with children, if they didn't like it they would have said 'On, no we have to go back'. But they didn't say that. They thoroughly enjoyed going back there and they thoroughly enjoyed singing with them ... I don't know what I expected. I really don't know. But it was better. I have never had a lot of contact with older people apart from parents or grandparents but you know, an old people's home ... But it was fantastic to see the children with the old people.

Teacher participants, Music for Life Project

Recommendations for intergenerational practice facilitators

As explored in this chapter, intergenerational projects can have a lasting impact on the subjective wellbeing of the participants and can encourage sustained lifelong learning and active ageing. Nonetheless, there are challenges that accompany intergenerational practice. As reported by facilitators in the Music for Life Project, these include differentiation and creating a sense of inclusion for all involved, finding appropriate repertoire, gaining the respect of the seniors, setting an appropriate pace for the sessions, and using appropriate language. These challenges could be overcome when the leaders and facilitators of intergenerational musical activities capitalize upon the strengths of the children and seniors alike.

Generativity would be supported if musical activities had some element built in where the older people are able to model for younger people 'the vitality that is possible to later life' (Rubinstein, 2002: 38), for example through collaborative musical games, collective singing, and also by offering opportunities for creativity through group improvisation or songwriting. In order for intergenerational musical activities to be inclusive, music facilitators should embrace frailty, not ignore it (Walker, 2008). Musical activities need to consider seniors' or children's physical or other limitations (Darrow and Belgrave, 2013) and run at a pace that allows seniors to interact with the vibrant and enthusiastic youth, yet allowing the children to encounter the life experience and emotional care and support offered by the seniors.

Lastly, intergenerational musical activities should encourage the participants' sense of autonomy and independence, both of which are very much sought and appreciated by children and seniors. Social affirmation and a sense of appreciation and belonging is experienced by the children when they are given the opportunity to take leadership and caring roles and to exercise their social skills (Darrow and Belgrave, 2013; Garber, 2004). For the older people this may be achieved through celebrating their prior knowledge as well as their new musical skills and by providing opportunities where they can model active ageing for younger people. Intergenerational practice is an ideal platform to model active ageing and lifelong learning, serving as a vehicle to bring about exchange of ideas between the generations.

Summary

The benefits of intergenerational music-making have been explored and discussed in this chapter, supported by narratives from the intergenerational programme of the Music for Life Project. Through intergenerational active music-making older people have the opportunity to model active ageing, contribute to meaningful and rich performance experiences for children and their families, encourage the dissolution of stereotypes, and leave a legacy of changed attitudes. Likewise, the children or young people can enhance the sense of purpose and social affirmation for the seniors and benefit themselves from interacting with a different generation that helps them to appreciate and prepare for active ageing.

Section Three

Supporting access to musical
participation amongst
older people

3

Chapter 8

Contexts for musical participation

This chapter is about the physical context of musical participation and its role in supporting inclusive, high quality practice. The physical context represents a learning environment that could be defined as 'all of the physical surroundings, psychological or emotional conditions, and social or cultural influences affecting the growth and development of an adult engaged in an educational enterprise' (Hiemstra, 1991). Where older people go to engage in learning activities varies greatly both in terms of the facilities available and physical and social accessibility. By social accessibility we refer to the extent to which a physical space fits an individual's expectations or sense of belonging. Spaces for engaging in learning activities vary greatly. Few are designed with adult learners in mind, particularly learners in the Third and Fourth Ages. We use examples from the Music for Life Project to demonstrate that issues relating to context contributed significantly to the experience of older people engaging in music activities. There has been very little written about the physical environment in relation to those engaging in activities in the Third and Fourth Ages; therefore the chapter draws on theory and research concerned with primary, secondary, and higher education, which can be applied to learners of any age.

The importance of context

The situational dimension of active ageing cannot be ignored. This dimension involves the geographical location of activities, characteristics of the physical space and resources, as well as the meanings that are conferred upon spaces. Armstrong (2012) claims that the ways that individuals use, imagine, and remember spaces are strongly linked with the experience of community-based adult education.

The role of 'place' in activities for older people may be important in a number of different respects. There are clear issues relating to contexts for participation being 'senior-friendly spaces' (Manheimer, 2009). In addition to physical barriers to participation, specific places may be associated with social values, power structures, or particular memories that might inhibit participation (Armstrong, 2012). In the case of activities that aim to promote wellbeing, there are issues concerning the extent to which the space may function as a 'therapeutic landscape' (Conradson, 2003). For example, it has been reported that three key dimensions of the physical environment that have a substantial influence on mental wellbeing are: the quality of the fabric of the physical environment; the ambient atmosphere, including lighting, heating, acoustics, colour; and the psychological environment, including perceptions of crowding and feelings of safety (GOScience, 2008). Finally, there are issues relating to 'spatial justice' (Armstrong, 2012), referring to fair and equitable access for older people to valued spaces that are conducive to learning and participation.

The importance of context for supporting engagement with learning amongst older people is discussed by Manheimer (2009). Describing the planning process for the North Carolina Centre for Creative Retirement, Manheimer emphasizes a sense of community and the importance and value attached to learning in later life, communicated in the design of this facility:

> The qualities of buildings that are elder-friendly, or as we would later call it, senior-friendly, of course included safety and comfort, but also much more ... the building should be user-friendly, and communicate openness and receptivity to program participants ... the architecture of the building ... [should] exude warmth and vitality ... The committee wanted newcomers to feel invited, welcomed, and uplifted; to know they can become part of an evolving community where they could make new friends, take initiatives to further their own learning goals and those of others.
>
> (Manheimer, 2009: 61)

While Manheimer's description may represent an ideal that is far from the reality of the spaces where many older people around the world congregate, there are important messages about how the context can play a vital part in supporting active participation in later life.

Places to learn

Adult education takes place in a variety of venues, many of which were not designed for that purpose. Taking the Music for Life Project as an example, one venue was an iconic, purpose-built arts centre whilst other sessions took place in the lounge areas of sheltered housing (assisted living). This is not to suggest that one venue was automatically better than another. Rather this highlights the important of 'place' as part of the experience of engaging in learning activities. As one choir member commented, 'the venue makes all the difference'.

Little has been written about physical space and its impact on older learners, compared with the literature concerned with environmental factors in schools and universities. However, learning landscapes, and specifically the redesign or reinvention of university classrooms, has been the focus of some academic research (Neary *et al.*, 2010). A theoretical framework that has been used for this is critical pedagogy (Freire 1970), an educational movement that aspires to raise student consciousness of authoritarian structures, with the aim being to break down hierarchical social structures of classrooms. In a similar vein, Gruenewald (2008: 320) proposes a 'critical pedagogy of place', challenging all educators to consider the 'social and ecological contexts' of their work, while Kuh *et al.* (2005: 106) argue that 'through buildings, signs, and the landscape of the campus, the physical environment communicates messages that influence students' feelings of wellbeing, belonging, and identity'.

The Joint Information Systems Committee (JISC, 2006) refers to the qualities that enhance learning in further and higher education, albeit with a focus on e-learning. These qualities of learning spaces include being flexible, creative, bold, and supportive:

> A learning space should be able to motivate learners and promote learning as an activity, support collaborative as well as formal practice, provide a personalised and inclusive environment, and be flexible in the face of changing needs.
>
> (JISC, 2006: 3)

Comparable qualities are referred to by Oblinger (2006), with some additional factors such as comfort and sensory stimulation for higher education students. With specific reference to school libraries, Susan La Marca (2010: 5) adds that 'Flexibility is the key to a learner-driven, human-centred environment ... spaces that are kept open and uncluttered, where all fixtures, furniture, technology, resource storage etc. [are] kept as simple and versatile as possible'. She also refers to essential features that include health-and-safety considerations, lighting, acoustics, temperature and air quality, and furniture. Similarly, James Pappas (1990) discusses the idea of a learning sanctuary in relation to conference venues. Conference organizers make use of spaces designed for other purposes, which may be university rooms, conference centres, or hotels. The environmental factors referred to are the amount of space, lighting, temperature, noise, décor, and furniture, all of which influence the affective experience of and cognitive outcomes for participants.

The educational environmental psychology of schools and day-care centres is discussed by Gifford (1997). Research is reported confirming that physical features of the learning environment do influence outcomes. Size is one important factor, with smaller schools faring better when it comes to student involvement in activities. In larger schools students tend to be spectators more than active participants. Another factor is attractiveness, which associates with better grades, but this is a subjective judgement making it difficult to suggest what an attractive learning setting might be. Similarly, preferred climate (including temperature, humidity, and air circulation) varies between individuals, although slightly cool, non-humid conditions have been found to promote learning. Seating arrangements and use of space are also influential, with groups around tables leading to greater interaction and less disruption compared to sitting in rows. Regarding the feelings engendered by physical contexts, students express preferences for softer, more home-like environments than tends to be the case in most schools and colleges. Gifford reports a study of a 'soft classroom', which showed that fears of damage were unfounded and that performance improved.

Environmental features such as those noted above may be particularly important with regard to spaces for older adult learning and participation, where many participants, for example, will have some extent of loss in visual acuity and hearing, as well as reduced mobility and other physical constraints. For music groups it is particularly important that spaces are large enough for the sound to resonate, lighting is strong enough to assist with reading notation, and seating is suitable for playing instruments. Although there has been little research with older people that has focused directly on these issues, the literature concerning physical and cognitive constraints and barriers to learning (see Chapters 3, 4, and 9) certainly would suggest that for those in the Third and Fourth Ages, the physical space may have a great influence on access and engagement with activities.

Before learning can occur, a basic requirement is the feeling of safety and inclusion, according to Strange and Banning (2001). The idea is based on Maslow's theory (1954) that social and cognitive needs depend on physical needs being met first. According to this theory, before meaningful engagement with learning activities could take place, buildings and rooms need to be accessible and promote a feeling of safety, particularly in poor weather or in the darker, winter months. This is a particularly salient issue for older people (see Chapter 9).

Physical environments are also associated with traditions and are therefore bearers of socio-cultural information. Jacobi and Stokols (1983: 159) refer to the 'social imageability of the physical environment – the capacity of places to evoke vivid, widely held social meanings among their occupants'. At certain times individuals will be more aware of the features of an environment and their symbolic meaning, but at others the 'aesthetic, functional, personal, or nonhistorical elements' will come to the fore (Jacobi and Stokols, 1983: 166). For example, rehearsing for a musical event in a concert hall can feel very different to rehearsing in other venues, or the actual performance.

Social accessibility is more subtle than whether the building is near public transport and has a lift, ramp, or good lighting. 'Physical structures themselves can be seen as artifacts that communicate nonverbally' (Strange and Banning, 2001: 23). Values and expectations are implicit in the physical environment. Negative first impressions may be erroneous but could be sufficient to prevent an individual staying with a programme. Other members of a learning group, who are part of the physical environment, can also signify whether the activity is deemed to be appropriate for an individual, influenced by first impressions or by preconceptions if the others are already known to the newcomer. Resources are also part of the physical environment, which for music activities might include audio-visual equipment and instruments. All of these elements hold socio-cultural meaning.

Many of those in the Third and Fourth Ages attending group music sessions will be reminded of experiences of education at an earlier age. These may be good or less good memories of school music lessons or learning instruments outside of school (see Chapter 6). In other words, older learners come with more 'baggage', as one might say, and that will include knowledge and experience of physical environments. Furthermore, older learners have chosen to attend, unlike those in compulsory education. They have the freedom to leave, should they be dissatisfied. Older learners may have more confidence, depending on the roles they have had in life, or conversely they may be under-confident and more susceptible to environmental factors that they perceive negatively. Pappas's proposal regarding conference centres holds true for adult learning:

> Thus, the continuing educator should be aware that participant reports of excitement, happiness, pleasure, boredom, or hostility to their experience directly reflect on the setting and the program [*sic*]. Consequently, continuing education programmers should be aware that they are seeking to direct or alter moods, that is, the affective quality of the participants' experience in the learning sanctuary.
>
> (Pappas, 1990: 47)

The use of space

In addition to the physical characteristics of a venue, the way that space is organized has been found to influence engagement with learning. Individual mood, self-concept and affective state can be influenced by the setting and by objects and others within that setting (Conradson, 2003). Lim *et al.* (2012) refer to this as 'spatial pedagogy'. From this perspective, different spaces within learning environments, as well as the patterns of movement and interaction within those spaces, acquire particular meanings. Lim *et al.* propose one framework for understanding the use of space, suggesting that the 'front-centre' of a classroom typically functions as an 'authoritative space' from which teachers deliver instructions and operate in a directive mode. A 'supervisory space' is where the teacher travels amongst the students, observing student work, while an 'interactional space' is where the teacher mingles with the students, interacting and problem-solving together, often accompanied by humour or casual banter. Finally, 'personal space' is typically located behind the desk, where the teacher organizes his or her materials. Their detailed analysis of two teachers' interactions with a junior college class revealed that the effects of use of space were mitigated by the interpersonal style and non-verbal dynamics of the teacher. Furthermore, their study demonstrated that different spaces could be used in such a way as to deliberately create a structured informality, contributing to a non-threatening learning environment. These studies have important messages for facilitators of groups of older people. The dynamic use of space on the part of the facilitators may be a particularly important strategy for creating a welcoming space for learning when working with individuals who may be restricted in mobility.

To summarize, theory and research has focused more on schools and universities than on spaces used for adult education programmes. Education-focused, purpose-designed and built institutions such as universities or arts centres function differently in comparison with spaces that are used because they are conveniently situated or available. Activities for older learners take place in a range of venues that vary in their suitability for learning activities and in their physical and social accessibility.

There are music programmes running in care homes, such as Musica (2013) in the South West of England, and First Taste (Fraser, 2006) in Derbyshire. These must work with the facilities available. Rooms used for music activities often have multiple purposes and might be shared, thus being available to other residents who may not wish to participate in music activities. Consequently, flexibility is not guaranteed, in spite of it being deemed to be an important quality for learning spaces. On the other hand, there are some similarities between sheltered housing or residential homes and university campuses or other educational establishments because a range of daily activities can take place in both, with designated areas for eating, drinking, and socializing. In addition to considerations relating to the physical space, the dynamic use of space within any venue can contribute to an informal and non-threatening environment that encourages participation. Wherever activities take place, the physical context is a fundamental, if often taken for granted, part of learning experiences.

In the next section, the physical contexts of the Music for Life Project will be described, followed by illustrative examples from the project of the facilitators' and participants' views on the learning environments and their influence on access to music activities.

Where musical activities took place in the Music for Life Project

The venues for the music activities in the Music for Life Project were situated in Gateshead near Newcastle in the North East of England and at a number of sites in London. The brief descriptions that follow serve to highlight the difference between the venues, in scale, purpose, and design.

Sage, Gateshead

The magnificent construction that is the Sage, Gateshead, was designed by Norman Foster and partners, and completed in 1994. It has won 13 awards (Foster and Partners, 2013). This is how the building is described by the venue's website:

> Designed by Lord Foster on a landmark waterfront site, Sage Gateshead incorporates outstanding performance spaces of internationally acclaimed acoustic excellence (Hall One and Hall Two), Northern Rock Foundation Hall for rehearsal and performance, a twenty-five room Music Education Centre, The Barbour Room (a sunny entertainment room), plus four bars, The Sir Michael Strake Café and The Brasserie.
>
> … The spectacular curved steel roof, which weighs in at 750 tonnes, is made from 3,000 stainless steel panels and 250 glass panels. If the roof were laid flat, its 12,000 square metre area would be big enough to accommodate two football pitches.
>
> Sage Gateshead, 2013

Other venues (outreach centres) used by the Silver Programme at the Sage, Gateshead, include Gateshead Old Town Hall (a restored Grade 2 listed building that opened in 1870), community centres, and church halls.

Guildhall Connect

The two venues for this programme of music activities were sheltered accommodation (assisted living) in East London. Each of the buildings housed approximately 30 flats, with communal spaces where the music activities took place. Before the sessions the musicians would clear furniture and make space in the centre for a circle of upholstered chairs, where the music-makers were seated. Other objects in the rooms indicated their multi-purpose nature: a kitchen area, a bird in a cage, a fish tank, some plants, photos from social events, a computer, television, and some drawings that residents had made. Both venues had a lift, although one participant needed someone to help with taking her wheelchair from her flat to the communal area, which was not always possible.

Westminster Adult Education Service (WAES)

At the time of the Music for Life Project, WAES used a number of sites for musical activities; however, it should be stated that WAES music activities subsequently moved to new, upgraded facilities in London. One location for music, at the time of the project, was a former school. A Victorian 'red brick' building, it was in a poor state of repair and was not deemed of sufficient interest to prevent its subsequent demolition. A lift ascended to various teaching rooms, off long corridors. The choir took place in a teaching room with long, rather high windows, typical of Victorian schools. Plastic chairs were placed in a semicircle. The keyboard was one that could be moved from one room to another. Aside from this, there were some tables around the edge of the room and some cupboards. As with the communal areas of sheltered housing, objects in the room (notably a life-size model skeleton) indicated its multipurpose use. The keyboard class was in a smaller room, with approximately ten keyboards placed on tables around the outside and down the middle of the room. There was a piano, a whiteboard and projector, and a computer.

Additional WAES musical activities that were specifically for older learners took place in a community centre run by Age UK, housed in a recently built, terraced building. A lift, if required, took participants up one floor to the social room. There were stackable dining-style chairs and tables placed in a line along the middle, conference style. On one wall was a very large flat-screen television. Older residents in the area could walk or use a mobility scooter to reach the centre for activities and lunch.

Finally, some musical activities hosted by WAES took place at an eight-storey block of sheltered housing that was built in 1969 and contained over 200 small flats. A lift took participants up to the eighth floor where there was a social area and kitchen. The social area was a large space with a piano and a range of comfortable, upholstered chairs. The windows on two sides of the room had far-reaching views over this area of London.

People in learning places – the Music for Life Project

Facilitators and participants who were interviewed for the project were asked a number of questions about their running of or participation in music activities. They were rarely asked directly about venues but there were references, nonetheless, that indicated the importance of place in their experiences.

> I think it'll be fine here, it's a nice room and everything so I think if people come across they'll think oh it's nice here.
>
> Pete, facilitator, Music for Life Project

> Some of the halls we are in are not very nice, depressing ... That's why I have stopped [attending a singing group] really ...
>
> Donna, aged 73, Music for Life Project

> This is a place that I feel it is a bit special and you treat people with love there.
>
> Corrine, aged 78, Music for Life Project

Impressions

There were very positive views of the Sage, Gateshead (SG), with participants and facilitators appreciating the fine building and the impressive combination of facilities within. The use of superlatives to describe it was noticeable compared with the mildly pleasant or less pleasant words used to describe other venues. The participants and facilitators described SG or their response to it in very positive terms: 'Staggering', 'Brilliant', 'Swept away', 'Fabulous', 'Fantastic', 'Great', 'You feel special, important', 'Welcoming', 'Very pleasant', 'Gives you a buzz'.

However, the grand scale of SG highlighted some of the advantages of other venues as well as individual preferences. One impression was that the building attracted a particular social class, could be intimidating, and was therefore potentially socially exclusive (Box 8.1).

Box 8.1 AN ARTS CENTRE AND OUTREACH CENTRES

Participants from the Sage, Gateshead spoke about their experience of the iconic arts centre, comparing this with an outreach centre:

> I feel it is quite a middle class place ... once went to a [local] women's choir and the ladies who were there ... might have felt uncomfortable in a group like this because they just think 'well, I am not like, you know, those ladies' and quite a lot of us had quite a lot of education and I wonder for some people if they just think 'I couldn't go in there and join that because I am not.'
>
> May, aged 76, Music for Life Project, Choir

> I personally prefer to rehearse here [Church Hall]. This is better to sing in acoustically than the rehearsal room in the Sage. And the caretaker lady here is brilliant. She is floating backwards and forwards. I mean, what started as making a cup of tea available for the groups in-between rehearsals, they are now bringing sandwiches, homemade cakes, and so on and so forth, so people are coming here and having their lunch.
>
> Hettie, aged 78, Music for Life Project, Choir

Getting there

Although many of the participants were able to walk, drive, or take public transport to the activities, there were some with mobility problems. Lifts were invaluable for accessing some rooms, for those people. However, some relied on others to help them and this led to occasional difficulties. For example, Joan was dependent upon assistance, not always forthcoming, in order to negotiate her wheelchair from her ground-floor flat to the room where the music activity was held. In some centres, participants were reliant on arranged transport, although occasionally that went awry and therefore reduced the number attending. Participants valued spaces that were accessible, particularly as this preserved a sense of independence. For example, Sam could participate in a musical group in the local centre, rather than relying on his wife to drive him elsewhere.

> I guess there are [other music groups]. It would mean me travelling somewhere and relying on my wife … No I enjoy what I have here and appreciate it.
>
> Sam, aged 83, Music for Life Project, Singing group

The Sage, Gateshead, was reported as being easily accessible by public transport, which was free for the over 60s. However, this was not true for all. Some people who did not live on a bus route found public transport to be no help. While some were fortunate enough to have cars, driving was challenging in poor weather or in the dark (Box 8.2).

BOX 8.2 ACCESSIBILITY OF SPACES

Participants in the Music for Life Project activities spoke about travelling to their groups. It was important that venues were accessible by public transport, and that activities were scheduled during daylight hours:

> We can travel here safely – there is a reasonable public transport here. It's a hub for the region here so all the public transport goes either to Newcastle or Gateshead. And then we'll have the yellow buses that are running around. They are the links that run around, so they are pretty frequent – less than 10 minutes between buses.
>
> Mark, aged 74, Music for Life Project, Guitar group

> It's not very convenient for me, it's one hour. I don't live locally. So if it is a night in winter, then I wouldn't come, in winter night I wouldn't come.
>
> Brenda, aged 77, Music for Life Project, Choir

Joining in

Physical context can, to a greater or lesser extent, be inviting. This has been interpreted as 'social accessibility'. Part of the physical context is the presence of other individuals. Many of the participants in the Music for Life Project had been or became friends with others who were involved with musical activities. However, in the more closed environment of the communal spaces in sheltered accommodation, there was some tension between the residents. This points to one potential advantage of having a third space, away from the social norms of a particular building, where established interpersonal tensions may interfere with establishing a positive environment for learning together (Box 8.3).

BOX 8.3 INTERPERSONAL ISSUES IN COMMUNAL RESIDENTIAL SPACES

I know why some tenants don't come down to the day room. It is because of other tenants ...

Marcy, Sheltered Housing Manager

They're sometimes arguing with each other, like someone said something that's upset someone and some argument is ensuing and I can just feel 'Oh no what's happened', it's like it's fragmenting and there's that gang over there who will say 'he said this' and 'he was so rude', so it does feel precarious, I suppose I feel it is sort of down to me, not to keep the peace, but keep a positive atmosphere.

Pete, Facilitator, Music for Life Project

[Some] are quite controlling of other people who are just frailer and sort of want to say what they can do when they can very well easily speak for themselves.

Janie, Facilitator, Music for Life Project

However, one advantage of multi-purpose, familiar venues was that that this encouraged some to join who may not otherwise have thought of being part of a musical activity. For example, two participants at one centre had been sitting outside while the music activity was on. Because there was a glass panelled wall with soft blinds and a glass door dividing the room from the corridor, these people could partially see in and be seen, thereby breaking down the boundary between those who were participating and those who were not. On the other hand, multiple uses of a room were not always conducive to a positive learning environment. This might be for the reason mentioned (interpersonal conflict), but in addition some activities do not combine well (Box 8.4).

Box 8.4 Multi-purpose Rooms

Yes, I used to sit outside the door listening to the music until I got caught! Pete said 'come in'.

Wendy, aged 78, Music for Life Project, Singing group

I was attending the club and because at that time everything was on the same floor. You had your coffee, tea there, so I listened to it one day and I just loved it.

Maureen, aged 79, Music for Life Project, Singing group

Those two things [music activity and people wishing to chat together] shouldn't be in the same room. They were having a cup of tea and talking. It's better now because we've got a second room.

Facilitator, Music for Life Project, Singing group

Use of space

The use of space varied amongst different types of groups, although it was noticeable that seating positions generally remained constant, whether sitting at a table, in a semicircle, dotted around the room or at keyboards. Indeed, this consistency in the use of space seemed to be particularly important for participants, with change sometimes being problematic (Box 8.5).

Box 8.5 Consistency in the use of space

In this hall here we found the lighting wasn't good for the pans; the way it shone – we couldn't see the notes very well. But it was also our first effort and at that time we seemed confused because we were all at different places to where we usually are when we are practising. We hadn't had a rehearsal facing the other way and being in different positions.

Mary, aged 78, Music for Life Project, Steel pans group

Figure 8.1 demonstrates that some groups were seated in a formal fashion, with the facilitator at the front (sometimes on a raised podium, for large groups), occupying what Lim *et al.* (2012) might refer to as an 'authoritative space'.

Others achieved a structured informality, with participants seated around a table or in semicircles. In the steel pan and keyboard groups, the facilitators often occupied a 'supervisory space', moving from one participant to another, observing, and assisting where required. The facilitators of recorder groups, rock groups, and some singing groups differed in that they made more use of an 'interactional space', making music alongside the participants as an equal member of the group (Lim *et al.*, 2012).

To a large extent, the size of group dictated the use of space, with very large groups in particular adopting formal seating in rows. In choirs, places were designated by singing voices, high or low, and in mixed choirs this would separate men from women.

However, the layout of the group did not always correspond with levels of interaction amongst peers. In some groups seated in circles there was little peer interaction, while in other groups seated in more formal rows there were many examples of peer interaction and support. Where facilitators made full use of space, alternating between an authoritative, supervisory and interactional space, groups were drawn in to the activity. Overall, the facilitator's interpersonal style and dynamic use of the space seemed to be key factors in engaging the older people in their music-making, in some cases mitigating constraints such as very large groups or difficult physical layouts.

Resources

Some of the venues were very well resourced. However, resourcing was problematic in other centres, for example with pianos that suffered from lack of tuning or being placed in hot rooms. Venues that had multiple purposes rather than being designed for musical activities had limited storage for instruments and this had direct consequences. For example, considerable time was spent setting up for activities, moving chairs and tables, retrieving a keyboard from another room or from storage, and setting up other instruments. Where storage was unavailable, resources were sometimes brought in by participants and often by facilitators. For example, one participant brought in a portable amplifier and microphone because he wished to amplify his voice when singing solos. Facilitators often brought instruments with them to their sessions and at one centre the facilitator had supplied a piano (Box 8.6).

Figure 8.1: Use of space among different types of groups

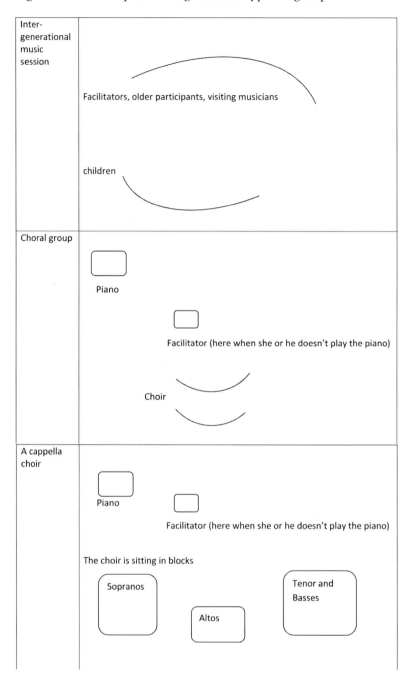

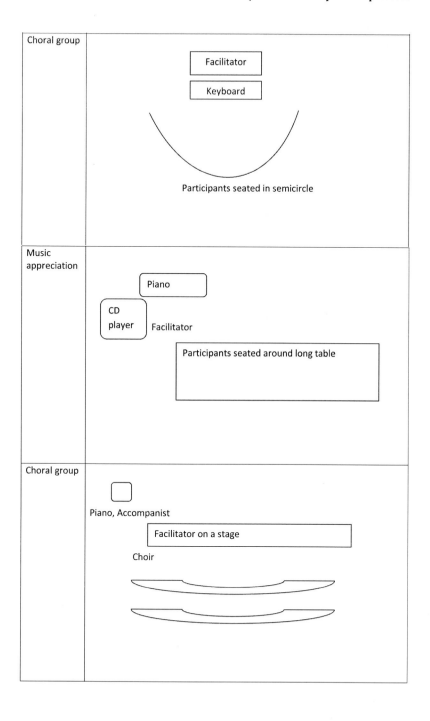

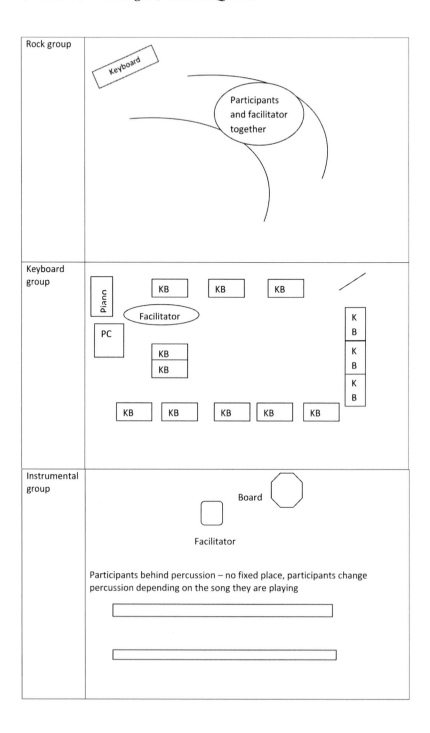

BOX 8.6 RESOURCE ISSUES – FACILITATORS' PERSPECTIVES

We weren't in a music room, we were actually in the sewing room, so at the beginning of each class we had to set up, we had to get all the keyboards out, we had to make sure there were no pins or needles around, which there invariably were, and the tables were the right height for sewing but the wrong height for keyboards, it was a bit of nightmare.

Helen, Facilitator, Music for Life Project

They didn't have a piano before I bought this piano. There's a pile of junk in the corner but it's about two semitones down, very bad.

John, Facilitator, Music for Life Project

They're all my instruments so it depends how much I can carry really. It would be nice to have an in-house set. It would be nice to have, they're all hand-held things, sometimes I've brought a xylophone, but I think I don't make any apologies for using these percussion instruments. They're real instruments and the music they produce is real music, but it would be nice to have a proper full-size xylophone with a nice tone to it.

Pete, Facilitator, Music for Life Project

Unsurprisingly, instruments that were brought for each session were restricted to what could be carried easily and consisted of simple percussion instruments. Whilst good use was made of these and some participants enjoyed playing them, others indicated that they found these instruments to be childish. There were further resource issues for participants in instrumental groups, who raised issues about access to instruments for practising. For example, in one centre there was a learning centre for those studying paper-based or computer courses but no practice room with instruments for use between sessions – a problem for those without an instrument at home (Box 8.7).

BOX 8.7 RESOURCE ISSUES – PARTICIPANTS' PERSPECTIVES

I don't like all this business of participating with tambourines and instruments; I find it a little bit childish.

Celia, aged 76, Music for Life Project, Singing group

We've got about two people who don't like [percussion instruments] ... they think it's going back to kindergarten, and we're talking about ladies in their late seventies and eighties and they just don't – to feel like you're being treated like children and I understand that, and I sort of have a bit of that myself but I overcome it because I think well this is something else to do. I don't have a tambourine in my life otherwise, or a maraca.

Betty, aged 79, Music for Life Project, Singing group

We haven't got spare keyboards where we can work anytime to practise. Some of us doesn't have keyboards, I have one but some people don't.

Brenda, aged 71, Music for Life Project, Keyboard group

Home comforts

Places for learning are equally important as social spaces for older people (see Chapter 2 for a full discussion of the importance of social networks). 'They do a very good lunch' (Sam, aged 83) is indicative of the many unprompted references to home comforts and catering facilities by participants from all of the venues (Box 8.8). Related to this was the size of the group, with some participants expressing a preference for smaller groups that promoted a family-like atmosphere.

BOX 8.8 SPACES FOR SOCIALIZING

And it's a good place to come and spend the day here if they want to. I don't usually but some people come for the day. And they have their lunch here and they have friends here.

Mark, aged 71, Music for Life Project, Guitar group

Then there is a half hour break, they come out and have their lunch and if people for the second session come a bit early and they have their lunch at the same time. That's why it is a madhouse. But they are very nice indeed, very pleasant, very amenable.

Sarah, aged 72, Music for Life Project, Choir

This gives you a buzz. It is lovely coming here even if you are not singing. You know, I go to the library, I come to the cafe.

Christine, aged 70, Music for Life Project, Choir

It has become too big now, so the groups are enormous so you've lost a little bit of something, you know ... At one time we were small, we knew each other and now we just feel it's so big. That we are losing a little bit of the intimacy which we like very much.

Carla, aged 76, Music for Life Project, Choir

Summary: the importance of context in music activities for older people

The examples from the Music for Life Project support the notion that the physical context is more than a container for activities. Specific contexts provide socio-cultural information about what is expected of facilitators and participants. Beyond practical issues such as storage of instruments or ease of access, each physical context fosters a feeling of some kind, whether that is awe or comfort or pride or a myriad other emotions. This corresponds with Conradson's (2003) idea that objects and space can influence one's self-concept and affective state.

It has been shown that the physical context, size of the group, and the use of space can function as inducements or equally as barriers to participation. Lack of access to quality facilities is certainly one barrier to participation and might indicate the low priority given to activities that can enhance the physical, cognitive, emotional, and social wellbeing of older people (see Section 1 of this book). Careful attention needs to be paid to the kinds of physical resources that are allocated for older people, ensuring that, as Armstrong (2012) would advocate, there is spatial justice, with equitable access to valued buildings and spaces. In particular, the difficulty of resourcing activities in non-specialized locations has been highlighted, as have the implications for the nature of the musical experience. Notwithstanding this, facilitators can mitigate the physical constraints of some venues through the dynamic use of the room, taking care to alternate between authoritative, supervisory, and interactive spaces (Lim *et al.*, 2012).

To conclude, the physical context is inextricably bound-up with the experiences of those attending music activities. Of course, the subjectivity involved in perceptions of physical contexts means that different venues can offer unique opportunities for accessing music activities, meeting a variety of different needs. Nonetheless, the physical context is so fundamental to the experience of those within it that it should be given serious consideration when planning or reviewing opportunities for older learners.

Chapter 9

Barriers to participation

This chapter focuses on the potential barriers to participation in musical activities, identified by participants, facilitators, programme organizers, and members of the wider community. Implications for policy and practice, including examples of strategies for overcoming structural, informational, social, and personal/dispositional barriers are highlighted.

Engagement in learning in musical contexts for older people

As discussed in Chapters 3 and 6, there is now an acknowledged, strong rationale for enabling older people to participate in all kinds of learning (Boulton-Lewis, 2010; Withnall, 2010). This rationale includes arguments relating to active ageing and comprises issues such as inclusion, social engagement, cognitive wellbeing, and enhanced physical and psychological health (Department of Health, 2001; Department of Work and Pensions, 2005, 2008; Audit Commission, 2008). Previous chapters in this book have demonstrated how musical activities represent one context for learning that has powerful potential for cultivating these promised benefits. However, questions remain with regard to how participation can be widened and barriers to participation overcome.

Previous research concerned with participation in learning amongst older people (including studies concerned with participation in music) has suggested that those most likely to access informal learning opportunities have relatively high levels of prior qualifications, are female, and are in good health (Aldridge and Tuckett, 2010; Cohen *et al.*, 2006; Jenkins and Mostafa, 2012). The findings from the Music for Life Project support this previous research, in that participants were predominantly female, white, and from professional occupations. Clearly, there are particular groups of people who are under-represented in organized musical activities for later-life learners. However, the problem may be related to recruitment, rather than retention. Findings from the Music for Life Project suggested that those who did participate continued their engagement into the Fourth Age. This could be attributed to sustained autonomy, control, and social affirmation, which were supported by the musical activities, creating an ongoing positively reinforcing cycle (see Chapter 2). Continued engagement with music may also have been a reflection of the view that retired people typically maintain their engagement in the same activities over time (Cohen *et al.*, 2002; Bungay and Skingley, 2008). The activities also provided a regular commitment, purpose, social support, challenge, and enjoyment for those who reported recent major life changes, such as retirement or bereavement.

Barriers to learning and participation

According to Duay and Bryan (2008), who carried out a qualitative study of 36 older-learners, learning in later life is experienced as being different from learning earlier in the lifecourse, with differences attributed to changes in physical and cognitive functioning, accumulated life experiences, and changes in motivations underpinning participation. Barriers to learning can therefore include psychosocial factors such as fear of failure, reluctance to engage with unfamiliar tasks, and perceptions of the complexity of the procedures required to join learning groups (Withnall, 2010). Other barriers include situational factors, those relating to the social or physical environment, institutional factors relating to the extent to which institutions exclude particular groups of learners, and informational barriers, relating to the efficiency of communication about learning opportunities (Darkenwald and Merriam, 1982). For example, the UK Audit Commission (2008) identified information barriers in Local Authorities, whereby older people were often found to lack access to information about interesting and worthwhile activities.

Some insight with regard to barriers to participation in music is provided by Keaney and Oskala (2007), who analysed the Taking Part survey in the UK, a major national survey that explored adult participation in the arts. The data collected from adults aged 55+ revealed that 'despite the declining rates of overall engagement, adults aged over 65 demonstrate continuing interest in the arts, with high rates of participation in a range of arts or arts-related activities' (Keaney and Oskala, 2007: 339). However, there were pronounced lower rates of engagement amongst men, as well as amongst older people with limiting health issues, older people from ethnic minority groups, and older people who lived alone. Survey respondents were asked to identify possible barriers to participation. Predictably, cost was one issue. Further frequently cited barriers were lack of social networks (see Chapter 2) and transport issues. Keaney and Oskala (2007: 350–1) point out that 'increasing engagement among the oldest age groups in particular may require creative ways of reducing the impact of poor health, lack of social networks, and lack of transport ... particular sub-groups within the older population may also require a targeted approach that tackles multiple barriers'.

Jansen (2005) explored barriers to participation in 'restorative activities', amongst community-dwelling elders. By 'restorative', Jansen refers to activities that enhance wellbeing through fostering a sense of 'being away', either physically in a new location or metaphorically allowing the mind to wander to another place. Restorative activities offer the scope for a person to 'feel in a whole other world', with his or her interest fully engaged and a high degree of 'fit and harmony' between the activity and the person's interests, wishes, and abilities' (Jansen, 2005: 37). An earlier piece of research (Jansen and von Sadovszky, 2004), exploring the types of activities that older people perceived to fulfil the qualities of 'restorative', had revealed that listening to music and playing musical instruments were experienced in this way.

In her follow-up study, Jansen (2005) interviewed 30 community-dwelling elders aged 65–92 (average age 75) about barriers to participation in restorative activities. The most frequently cited barriers were health limitations, lack of time, ageist attitudes, transportation difficulties, lack of a companion, and financial constraints. Some further barriers to participation were weather, limited opportunities, family separation, safety, and lack of space. Jansen noted that some ageist attitudes included attitudes that the participants themselves expressed about being old, with some self-limiting their activities because of perceptions they held about what it meant to be an older person. A range of strategies is proposed for addressing the barriers. Activities need to be wide-ranging and structured in such a way as to be responsive to the diverse preferences and needs of the elders. They also need to be within close proximity of older people's residences. Jansen also advocated 'leisure education' (increasing awareness of available activities and resources) and 'leisure counseling', addressing 'the physical, psychological, and social barriers that may influence an individual's attitudes and behaviours regarding leisure' (2005: 50).

Barriers to participation in music amongst older people

The Music for Life Project participants, facilitators, programme organizers and members of the wider community (relatives, sheltered housing managers, and representatives of charities who support older people) contributed to an understanding of the barriers that might prevent participation in music-making amongst older people. The overarching barriers to participation were categorized as structural, informational, social, or personal/dispositional.

Structural barriers

Structural barriers to participation included finance, location, timing, and transport issues. Participants in the Music for Life Project talked about barriers that they faced in relation to the cost of the music programmes and the physical access to various locations where the activities took place. Some potentially invisible barriers relating to location were identified, for example when musical activities were held in buildings with religious connections or in spaces that were perceived as being elitist and exclusive. For some participants, time of day was a crucial factor. Problems with location posed some problems, while the quality of the facilities was also a factor that considerably enhanced the overall experience of taking part, in particular contributing to a sense of participating in a valued and meaningful activity (see Chapter 8).

Similarly, issues raised by facilitators and members of the wider community included finance, location, and transport issues. Finding and protecting funding for musical activities with older people was seen as a challenge, exacerbated by a belief that in order to make the activities accessible, fees needed to be kept to a minimum. The three case-study sites had differing charging policies; participants at WAES were charged termly fees that were in some cases subsidized by the Personal Community Development Learning Fund. At the Sage, Gateshead participants paid a small charge per session on a 'pay as you go' basis. The Guildhall Connect Project did not charge for participation. Examples from the interviews are given in Box 9.1.

Box 9.1 Structural barriers to participation

Location: problematic access

My life is somewhat regulated by difficulty in walking.

Some people come on the train and they have to get the bus as well.

I am not in any other of the groups here mainly because of the distance. That's the only thing that is stopping me.

I think it is very important to have access to music/singing projects where people already meet.

There are choirs [not far away] and he doesn't really want to do that. Everything has to be on the doorstep.

The centre is fine, but the available studio is 'The Roof Studio' consequently there are many, many stairs to climb with no lift. Fine if one is totally fit. I don't know this can be overcome. We do not want to lose this accommodation and alas, new premises provision has been cancelled due to credit crunch.

Music for Life Project participants

Location: contributing to a sense of being valued

Venue is important for me because it is such a staggering [place]. It is staggering really when you walk in. The staff here are very, very good. The facilities are all here ... Everything is all set up.

The venue makes all the difference I think. ... you feel special. You feel important and you feel that it is for you.

Music for Life Project participants

Location – invisible barriers

First of all I have been afraid, well, maybe the venue was the church hall and maybe they are only thinking of Christian songs. But, no. Obviously in December we had to practise the Christmas carols because it is Christmas.

People are frightened of it [the arts centre] because they think 'Oh, we've got to pay money'. I said 'No, it's free, walk around, you know'.

It's not elitist. I think people think of the [arts centre] as this iconic building and off you go 'The [arts centre] is elitist', but it is not! Not at all.

It is perceived to be a classical music centre. The reality is if you get yourself through the front doors everybody is very welcoming.

Music for Life Project participants

Time of day

If it is a night in winter, then I wouldn't come.

They changed the day from Thursday to Wednesday, didn't they? ... And the other thing about this one is that it starts at half ten. Now, those people who have a little way to come – you can't get on the bus with your pass until half nine so then it's a little bit early.

I wish it was during the day, I really do, I feel I would get more out of it, too.

I don't like going out in the dark alone ...

Music for Life Project participants

Financial issues – cost

Adult education classes are becoming increasingly more expensive. There was a time when over 60s could attend many classes for just £1 (a term). This is/seems ridiculously cheap, but now classes can cost as much as £100 or more per term/year. Some people really cannot afford even this. I have to travel to participate so transport costs and parking are a problem.

The Silver programme at the Sage has been life-changing for many retired people, offering as it does tuition at a low cost.

A reasonable cost because guitar lessons for an hour would cost twenty to thirty pounds for an hour; this costs two pounds fifty.

I mean our greatest expense is the bus because you cannot use the bus pass before nine thirty.

I find the admin fee is very hard, twenty pounds. It used to be ten pounds.

If you're on benefit, or pension, you don't pay much.

I think for some people cost must be off-putting.

Music for Life Project participants

Facilities – negative

> It's a bit crowded. Too cramped. So when people come in
> or when you come late and you step on the microphones …
> It's not great but you know it could improve things. If
> someone took ten minutes or either give us a bigger room
> or get the room set up.
>
> Music for Life Project participants

Information barriers

A perceived lack of information and publicity for some programmes was
seen by participants as a barrier. For many, finding out about the activity they
were involved in had been serendipitous rather than as a result of a deliberate
search for information. Facilitators and other representatives of the wider
community also recognized difficulty with dissemination of information
as a potential barrier that needed to be addressed by those who organized
activities. Information, marketing, and outreach issues were raised. Ensuring
information reached all potential participants, particularly men, was seen
as being challenging. Given the importance of word of mouth, reported by
those supporting participation as well as participants, the gap between more
and less socially involved individuals was possibly a relevant issue. Example
statements are given in Box 9.2.

BOX 9.2 INFORMATION BARRIERS TO PARTICIPATION

More information and publicity

> I can't say I have seen many adverts outside of the [centre].
> I have been on the internet. There are things I found on the
> internet.

> It would be nice to have more, as I said it should have
> been advertised better. My library is the Paddington one
> and the Marylebone, my two libraries, and I didn't see it
> advertised there.

> It was a year after I retired that I actually saw this … I
> don't know why I wasn't aware of all that literature.

> I don't think they advertise it a lot. I wouldn't have known about it if I hadn't seen it in the booklet at the library. I found a leaflet just by accident.
>
> I do not think people in the community would be aware of music for older people unless it is well advertised in the area.
>
> I think many people in the community have not heard of music programmes for older people, although there are many established choirs in the area.
>
> We have a style of marketing which doesn't appeal to a lot of older people. It's too posh.
>
> I don't know how to add extra people from this building, they know we're here. We could make it more evident by putting up posters and putting a notice on the board, 'choir today', or 'today's the day for singing, please come up'.
>
> Music for Life Project participants

Social barriers

Many of the barriers raised by participants related to social roles, orientations, and commitments. Some spoke of competing commitments, particularly with regards to caring responsibilities. It was recognized that the significant contribution some older people made to their extended families as care-givers for grandchildren, in addition to responsibilities caring for older relatives, impacted on their availability for group participation.

Others articulated perceptions of music-making activities as not being aligned with their social roles or orientation, either because of gender, social class, or ethnicity. Men were much less likely to participate in the musical activities than women. While the participants rejected the idea that their experience of music-making had been elitist, they suggested that any such perception in the general community could be addressed through increasing participation amongst younger adults. Barriers relating to ethnic minority participation were recognized, although there was little sense amongst the responses of how activities might be structured in order to meet the needs of the groups who were not participating (see Box 9.3 for examples).

Box 9.3 Social barriers to participation

Caring for relatives

As a full time carer I sometimes find it difficult to attend all the classes I would like to.

The other thing increasingly taking their time up is grandchildren, very noticeable. There's no proper child care that's affordable for working people, you've got to have loads of problems to get cheap child care. If you're just a working person in London, you can't afford it, so granny or grandpa, or both, are called in.

Those who have care commitments (partners/grandchildren/parents) and those whose health is failing find it difficult [to come to the sessions] at times.

Music for Life Project participants

Social orientations – ethnic minority groups

I mean there is an Indian community but they will never come … it really sort of worries me a bit. I live in a community where lots of old Chinese will never come. Because they don't think they speak good English. But you don't have to speak good English. Maybe it's not their culture to join … so multi-culture, multi-racial country here and actually I was surprised when I joined the [choir] and I am the only one sort of minority background. [Japanese]

The women in particular don't do things on their own as much and certainly when I was teaching at the West End where there are all Asians and the women did not join things. They didn't do things. They stayed at home.

They tend to keep to themselves. Say, the Chinese community, they tend to have activities of their own. They tend to stick together. I don't know about the others but I know for a fact that their interests tend to revolve around their friends and their own group rather than joining in things.

> First generation immigrants don't usually join mainstream activities. You know, it's often third generation.
>
> Music for Life Project participants

Social class

> I also wonder how wide the participation is. Might be seen as a very middle class activity? Leisure activities should start with primary education.
>
> This is the greatest opportunity that I have ever had to express my musical talents. Before it always felt that it was an elitist sphere. Only at school was this encouraged, how sad the missing years must have been (without knowing).
>
> Music for Life Project participants

Personal and dispositional barriers

Personal and dispositional constraints were evident amongst participants from the sheltered housing accommodation, where tenants reported that their fellow residents were extremely reticent about joining-in with group activities. This reticence was attributed to lack of interest, a lack of willingness to socialize, or a lack of confidence. These issues were seen as being interrelated; for example, the perceived lack of confidence amongst participants could have been related to inhibition and greater isolation. In this vein, there was some frustration that fellow tenants were reluctant to participate, particularly when it was clear that some were isolated. In some cases, reticence on the part of the older people was interpreted as a lack of interest, with little appreciation of some further 'invisible' psychological barriers, although there was recognition that some irregular patterns of participation were attributable to physical illness or age-related changes in physical functioning (see Box 9.4 for examples).

Box 9.4 Personal and dispositional barriers to participation

Perceptions of lack of interest and unwillingness to socialize

> It's just people just aren't that interested, I think ... even if you go to these tenants meetings they are not always well represented. People just like to do their own things.

> They don't come even for the music. They don't come even to associate with us. I mean, we are thirty-four here and you see with your eyes, I mean, six or seven they come. They don't even come to associate. We don't know the people living here sometimes. You don't see them.
>
> Music for Life Project participants

Health

> ... or somebody else might be ill, you know. And that has stopped a few more people. We would be about three more only because of that. But that can't be solved.

> Difficulties: past throat nodules – limits what I would like; arthritic spine prevents involvement with drums!

> It's not age but physical injury – osteoarthritis – that stops physical activity.

> I haven't been to concerts for ages. No. Partly, because I wouldn't be all that comfortable sitting for a long while but I do like to listen to [concerts] on the radio.
>
> Music for Life Project participants

Reluctance to participate

> The community, you can get them out, keep talking to them but they don't want to. We have so many things going on, I mean the organizers really begged people to come out. I suppose they're set in their ways, some like the TV, they're sitting from morning till night with the television. Wherever we go, they're asking for people to join in.
>
> Music for Life Project participants

Lack of confidence

> The main barrier is self-confidence – having the guts to come out of the house to a new group of people.

> I think you would need to come with somebody maybe. And you might think, as well, 'I don't know how high the standard is', 'What if I am not good enough?'
>
> Music for Life Project participants

Lack of motivation

> There is a general feeling from what I can gather from the older people in our group that some people don't do anything and it's very hard to get them motivated to try stuff.

> Motivating for the first time is the hardest thing. That's why we've now got activity link workers which we got funding for.

> A lot of them are on their own, nobody at home's going to say what are you doing, you have to push yourself.
>
> Music for Life Project participants

Overcoming barriers

Music for Life Project facilitators and members of the wider community suggested a number of ways in which barriers could be overcome. Once participants had attended one or more sessions, the social and pastoral aspects of facilitation were described as crucial to continued participation in and enjoyment of activities. Facilitators reported that the participants themselves and their relatives could play an important part in this. In particular, a welcoming atmosphere characterized by trust and respect was seen as vital. Facilitators reported that this kind of welcoming atmosphere was achieved, in part, through organizing their sessions with time built in for socializing. Some groups designated 'buddy systems', with individual participants taking responsibility for helping newcomers integrate socially. Others had volunteer support, taking responsibility for following up any absentees, sending cards to those who were away because of illness, and generally helping to find solutions to potential barriers to participation. A crucial factor was that systems and strategies were in place that demonstrated to individuals that their contribution and participation really did matter.

It was also recognized that owing to a number of factors older participants might drop in and out of activities. Thus, facilitators needed to be able to accommodate irregular patterns of engagement and to help individuals to maintain a sense of being part of the group even when various constraints prevented them from regular attendance.

The physical location of musical activities and the quality of the facilities also made a difference. Apart from ensuring that the venue was warm, well-lit and equipped with suitable resources, one facilitator reported that access to 'prestigious' venues helped to raise their groups' collective sense of value and esteem (see Box 9.5 for examples).

Box 9.5 Suggestions for overcoming barriers

Being welcoming and inclusive

The central reason behind our success is, I feel, the pastoral care that we provide for our participants – they are always welcomed by a familiar face and we always make time to chat before and after a session.

It's not about going to ask them what is going on in their lives but I think just being open and being warm and being there before the session, being able to talk to them about what's happening is really important.

People need to know they are welcome and that solutions will be looked for, for any issues there may be.

Many groups are 'un-auditioned' so everyone is welcome.

Facilitator, Music for Life Project

Building and facilities

The rooms have good acoustics, good light, and the pianos are generally excellent. It's good to have such good catering facilities on site and the venue is warm and hospitable. The atmosphere is friendly, the building very accessible.

It's a big, shiny building and I think everybody knows it ... it's got prestige. I think again the cafe is good ... it's a place where people can meet socially. And there are soft chairs down the side where people bring their packed lunch, so it's a good social gathering place.

Facilitator, Music for Life Project

Reaching out: accommodating irregular patterns of participation

Demonstrating to participants that they matter; accommodating irregular patterns of participation; listening to participants' personal stories.

If a participant is absent for a few sessions ... it is followed up and our fantastic volunteer will get in contact to see if everything is OK. This is so important – it means that our participants feel valued and listened to, when in many cases this is not how they feel in their day-to-day lives.

Or they disappear, say sick husband, they could disappear for four years then come back again.

They feel attached to us because they keep getting the information, which is costly, but if you keep informing people they're reassured by knowing we're there if they need us.

If people haven't turned up for a few weeks we give them a ring and see, you know. And it's not an intrusive thing at all. We get a lot of people saying how much they appreciate getting a card when they are ill or things like that.

Facilitator, Music for Life Project

Suggestions made by facilitators as to how the barriers might be overcome included:

- holding taster sessions
- participants accompanying a friend
- user-friendly marketing
- making people feel welcome by meeting the needs of specific groups
- keeping costs low

- having public transport available
- taking activities to older people.

Those involved in the wider community made a range of further suggestions that would provide support and sustain interest. They suggested that provision should be:

- sustained
- offer progression
- offer enjoyment
- develop skills
- be safe
- provide opportunities for performance
- be inclusive.

The views of the Music for Life Project participants and facilitators were largely reinforced by feedback from a consultative conference of stakeholders, involving providers of lifelong learning, including music participation opportunities for older people, representatives from charities concerned with ageing, representatives from sheltered housing associations and representatives from the older people's groups. The predominant themes in the conference feedback suggested that the role of the facilitator was crucial in ensuring that music sessions with older people were effective and maximized the potential for positive outcomes. Interpersonal skills were regarded as paramount, as well as teaching skills, including the ability to apply differentiation strategies. These skills were considered to be of equal – if not greater – importance than sound musical knowledge and a good standard of musicianship

Many of the barriers identified (structural, informational, social, personal/dispositional) are common to all formal adult learning activities (Audit Commission, 2008; Darkenwald and Merriam, 1982; Withnall, 2010). The issue of perceived elitism may be particularly relevant for musical activities. Much informal musical provision for adults requires existing levels of musical expertise, although this is changing, with providers now offering activities for beginner instrumentalists and opportunities to sing, which do not require auditions. Opportunities to engage with a wider range of musical genres are beginning to emerge, catering for more tastes. Some, e.g. rock and pop music, seem to be particularly attractive to men, reflecting gendered preferences for certain kinds of instruments and genres throughout the lifespan (Hallam *et al.*, 2008), while lack of confidence can be ameliorated by open access community music projects (Hillman, 2002).

Given the benefits of active engagement in music, there is a need to find ways to facilitate greater access and widen participation. To increase participation, activities need to be in locations that are convenient and easily accessed and do not have religious or other connotations that may act to deter particular groups of people. Costs need to be kept to a minimum so that participation is affordable. Publicity needs to be targeted at those who are least likely to attend. For instance, flyers and posters could be displayed in health centres and local shops and supermarkets where there is broad representation of the wider population. To support those who lack confidence, current participants could be encouraged to act as buddies for reticent new recruits. The activities on offer need to be attractive to a broad group of participants, both in terms of ensembles and repertoire, with a welcoming atmosphere characterized by trust and respect. Opportunities for socializing and some pastoral support need to be incorporated in the activities. The music-making itself needs to be of a high quality, with credible music facilitators providing joyful and engaging musical activities that are responsive to the needs of specific groups (see Chapter 6).

Summary

A number of barriers to participation have been identified in previous research concerned with lifelong learning and participation in the arts, as well as research concerned with restorative activities, including music-making. Predominant barriers are cost, health, transport, and lack of companionship. For some older people, deeply rooted attitudes about what it means to be old acted as barriers to participation. Creative responses are required to address these issues that relate to social networks, health constraints, and location of activities. In particular, care must be given to ensuring that those with multiple barriers to participation are helped in accessing activities.

These broad findings were supported by participants, facilitators, and other stakeholders in the Music for Life Project. Various barriers were identified and discussed. Structural barriers were those that related to physical access to facilities, perceptions of the location as being too elitist, financial constraints and time of day. Information barriers were also identified; it was apparent that many participants had come across information about music sessions purely by chance and there did not seem to be any systematic knowledge or place that older people could access reliable information about what was available in their area. Some personal and social barriers were also identified, including caring responsibilities, social orientations and personal interest, willingness to socialize, confidence, and motivation.

Several suggestions were made with regard to how the barriers might be overcome. It was emphasized that music sessions needed to be welcoming and inclusive, led by facilitators who established mutually respectful communication and set purposeful, enjoyable tasks that took account of the prior experience their adult participants brought to the group. It was also thought that care had to be taken over ensuring that the physical context was accessible, for example taking music-making to the older people's residential sites, or making use of outreach locations. Finally, pastoral support (for example, 'buddy' systems, time for socializing) was thought to be an important element in helping individuals to develop confidence and motivation to attend group sessions.

Chapter 10
Conclusions

This chapter draws together the themes of active ageing, active participation in music, and wellbeing. Key points emerging from the background literature are summarized and interpreted within the framework set out by the UNESCO Seoul Agenda for music education. Finally, principles of active ageing and underlying dimensions of wellbeing will be summarized, with reference to key points emerging from the literature concerned with participation in music-making amongst older people. Implications and key messages are highlighted. These have relevance for:

- *older people who are interested in participating in musical activities*
- *care-givers who are interested in supporting older people with engagement in music*
- *facilitators of musical activities*
- *funders and policy makers with influence over 'arts for health' initiatives.*

Our overarching message is that music-making has the potential to function as a powerful vehicle that supports active ageing. The arguments and evidence set out in this book demonstrate that musical activities are holistic, in the sense that they involve emotional, cognitive, and physical engagement. Music-making in groups brings the added social context; musical social networks have been shown to support older people in practical ways, as well as contributing to sustained social and emotional wellbeing.

Coinciding with the extraordinary demographic transition that has made ageing a highly relevant political issue, there has been increasing interest in the power of music in the lives of older people. New initiatives have been developed within a range of contexts for older people, and researchers have investigated the relationship between music, wellbeing, and active ageing, from a number of perspectives.

Lifelong learning in music
Lifelong learning has been identified as one of the key determinants of active ageing (WHO, 2002). However, as noted in Chapter 5 of this book, policies and practices relating to lifelong learning in *music* remain under-researched and under-resourced.

Notwithstanding the growing interest in music, wellbeing, and ageing, there is still much to be done before access to the full potential of music might be a reality for our older generations. The United Nations Seoul Agenda for Development of Arts Education (UNESCO, 2010) provides a useful framework for a discussion of relevant issues. This document was produced following UNESCO's Second World Conference on Arts Education, following extensive consultation and input from 650 arts education experts representing 95 countries. An underpinning principle of the consultative process was that 'arts education can make a direct contribution to resolving the social and cultural challenges facing the world today' and further, that 'of crucial importance to the success of arts education in meeting these challenges is the need to achieve high standards in the conception and delivery of programmes' (UNESCO, 2010: 2).

Crucially, the Seoul Agenda enshrines the principle of *lifelong* learning, embedding this concept within the three overarching goals of access, quality, and social change. UNESCO Member States and constituent communities are called upon to take action with regard to these goals and associated action points, in order to benefit lifelong learners *of all ages* [p.2: italics added]. Several specific strategies and action points outlined in the Seoul Agenda are worthy of attention, with reference to their importance in furthering awareness of the importance of musical opportunities for older people.

Goal 1: Access

The Seoul Agenda stipulates that the principle of accessibility involves an affirmation of 'arts education as the foundation for balanced creative, cognitive, emotional, aesthetic, and social development of children, youth, and lifelong learners' (UNESCO, 2010: 3). We have argued that music-making offers a context where this balance of needs may be met (see Section 1 of this book). For older people, music may be particularly important in this regard. The Third and Fourth Ages are phases of life that have been characterized as periods of intense creativity, where individuals continue to have the need for, and an entitlement to, aesthetic experiences such as musical engagement. It has also been suggested that meeting the challenges of later-life transitions can be helped with engagement in activities such as music that contribute to sustained cognitive vitality and social-emotional wellbeing. In short, music is one activity that can meet many of our needs that continue to be salient throughout our lives – social, cognitive, creative, affective, and aesthetic.

The Seoul Agenda also stipulates that 'learners from all social backgrounds have lifelong access to arts education in a wide range of community and institutional settings' (UNESCO, 2010: 4). This point has important implications for older people. Interpreted in its most inclusive sense, the message is that arts educators should take account of people at all stages of the lifespan, within a wide range of contexts. Chapter 5 of this book outlined arguments in favour of the view that musical development and progression are entirely possible throughout our lives. For this reason alone, older people deserve opportunities to explore their musicality. When considered alongside the evidence that links music-making with social, emotional, and cognitive wellbeing (Section 1 of this book), the argument for active musical engagement amongst older people becomes even more compelling.

While the evidence presented in this book tells a powerful story about the role of music in older people's lives, it must be acknowledged that programmes and practices have some way to go before the picture of music provision for older people could be said to be truly inclusive. For example, representative diversity in socio-economic and cultural background has been lacking in much of the research. Furthermore, apart from some very valuable practice and research with older people living with dementia and some other age-related conditions, there has been little research that explores fully how music-making may be exploited within a range of community and institutional settings that reach the most vulnerable and frail of our older people. This point was addressed in Chapter 9 of this book, where barriers to participation are explored, and in Chapter 8, where issues were raised such as spatial justice, referring to equitable access to valued spaces and resources.

Goal 2: Quality

The second overarching principle of the Seoul Agenda is a commitment to arts education that is high quality in conception and in delivery. Chapter 6 of this book explored the implications of this issue for older people, with a discussion of how facilitators can best meet the needs of music groups comprising people in the Third and Fourth Ages. In order for musical activities to act as a pathway to sustained or enhanced wellbeing, as the evidence suggests is possible, provision must be of a high quality, responding to the diverse needs amongst older cohorts. To this end, there is a need for professional development for musicians, care-givers, and stakeholders with an interest in supporting activities for older people. Professional development opportunities would be strengthened through partnership working (e.g. across social, health, community, and musical sectors) as well as from exchange amongst researchers and practitioners. For example, First Taste, a UK charity that provides creative arts sessions for people in residential care, has built into its projects an element of research and evaluation, as well as embedding into the sessions professional development for care-givers (Fraser, 2006; 2009).

Goal 3: Social change

Issues relating to active ageing and wellbeing in later life affect us all. Indeed, an ageing population represents one of the major global challenges of the twenty-first century (see the Introduction to this book), requiring responses that help older people to remain active and healthy. The third overarching goal set out in the Seoul Agenda for Arts Education advocates for arts education as a medium for bringing about social change. With reference to the challenges related to ageing, the aspiration of social change aligns with arts initiatives that 'encourage recognition of the social and cultural wellbeing dimensions of arts education' as well as 'the therapeutic and health dimensions of arts education' (UNESCO, 2010: 9). Section 1 of this book sets out a range of evidence illustrating the ways in which musical engagement amongst older people can be transformational in a therapeutic sense, linking with personal and social wellbeing. In addition, Chapter 7 explored the potential for intergenerational musical activities to break down age-related stereotypes and promote intergenerational understanding and solidarity, to provide opportunities for cultural traditions and knowledge to be passed on, and to foster community engagement.

Active ageing through music

The 'worldwide triumph of population ageing' (WHO, 2002: 4) raises important questions relating to how we can support older people in leading independent and active lives, and provokes discussion and debate with regard to what sorts of initiatives can facilitate transitions into the Third and Fourth Ages. This book has focused on music-making as one domain of activity that offers powerful potential for addressing these challenges and helping older people to enjoy sustained wellbeing.

Active ageing has been linked with quality of life and has been conceptualized as a process that involves optimal opportunities for health, participation, and security throughout the latter stages of life (WHO, 2002: 12). There are several ways in which music-making has been shown to support active ageing. In addition to influencing positive mental and physical health (Section 1 of this book), music-making provides a context that promotes independence and self-fulfilment (Chapter 5), alongside interdependence and intergenerational solidarity (Chapter 7).

The active ageing framework proposed by the World Health Organization (2002) focuses on equality of opportunity at all points in the lifecourse, with a central tenet being the idea of continuing participation. From this view, active ageing requires that participation must be supported in such a way as to be inclusive of 'those who are frail, disabled or in need of care', meeting a range of needs, desires, and capacities. As noted above, there is still much to be done with regard to developing truly inclusive practice in music. Nevertheless, there is a strong rationale for directing resources into this work, as the universal nature of music means that it has the potential to reach diverse groups amongst older people and touch their lives in powerful ways.

According to the World Health Association framework (2002) there are several determinants of active ageing, amongst which are psychological factors. In this book we have illustrated several ways in which music might mediate a range of psychological determinants of active ageing. For example, Chapter 3 demonstrated some ways in which participation in music might compensate for declines in specific areas of cognitive capacity such as processing speed and short term memory, offering opportunities for engagement in cognitively challenging activities, as well as providing the scope for applying prior knowledge and experience.

Furthermore, as noted in Chapter 2, positive psychological benefits that have been attributed to music include reduced anxiety and alleviation of depression, emotional self-regulation, and communication. Active participation in making music has also been linked with increased confidence, creative expression, and feelings of accomplishment and empowerment. Similarly, Chapter 5 showed how music-making could provide a context where individuals experienced a sense of purpose and autonomy, as well as enjoyment and an understanding of coherence and continuity in one's life.

In addition to individual psychological factors, social support has been identified as a key determinant of active ageing (WHO, 2002). In this sense, music-making has much to offer. Engagement in musical social networks can be a joyful experience that counteracts loneliness and depression, both of which are major challenges associated with the Third and (particularly) the Fourth Ages. In Chapter 2 we explored the potential for musical social networks to support older people in practical and emotional ways, showing how musical groups provided a source of fellowship and helped individuals to remain connected to their communities, developing new role relationships and attachments.

A framework for understanding psychological wellbeing in old age was set out in the Introduction of this book and applied to examples of engagement with music-making, at various junctures throughout the book. This 'needs satisfaction' framework suggests that positive wellbeing is enhanced when activities contribute to a continuing sense of purpose and enjoyment – or what might be termed as *'joie de vivre'*. Positive wellbeing, according to this framework, is also supported when the view of oneself as being competent and in control in specific domains is reinforced, and when a sense of social affirmation, being both valued and cared for, is validated through activities where individuals contribute in a meaningful way. Throughout the book we have used the voices of older people themselves to demonstrate how their experience as music-makers fulfilled these needs and helped them to sustain positive wellbeing whilst negotiating challenges associated with ageing.

The World Health Organization (2002) advocates for initiatives that support positive gains with regard to the facets of wellbeing noted above. Initiatives with music-making at their core have the potential to function in exactly this way. Musical groups, supported by expert facilitators, offer a space where older people can develop self-efficacy, apply cognitive skills, and where their prior life experiences may be recognized and celebrated. Community music groups have the scope to be responsive to the capacities, needs, and desires of the constituent members. Groups that support intergenerational contact may be particularly important for addressing social isolation and promoting positive attitudes to ageing within the wider community.

However, we are careful to use the word 'potential', when discussing the relationship of music, ageing, and wellbeing. In order for the positive benefits that have been noted to be maximized, careful thought needs to be given with regard to overcoming barriers to participation and ensuring that music-making opportunities are inclusive. Chapter 9 of this book explored potential barriers to participation. In addition to visible barriers such as transport, finance, care-giving responsibilities, and features of the physical environment, there may be a range of invisible barriers that relate to cultural stereotypes, confidence, and prior experiences that influence expectations or generate anxiety about participation.

Furthermore, whilst we argue in favour of the view that there is a strong link between psychological factors, musical engagement, and active ageing, we acknowledge that further research is needed to support the case for significant investment in policies and programmes that promote music-making amongst older people. Whilst delivering powerful messages, many of the studies cited in this book have been relatively small scale and, as noted above, limited with regard to the representative nature of research participants. Notwithstanding this, the words of older people who have reported significant benefits should not be ignored:

> It's the most uplifting thing that you can do actually … anything
> that is troubling you, any problem you have is completely forgotten

when you get in here … It keeps me active, alert and organized …
Simply the joy it brings into my life … It has been very positive and
encourages one to do more things and it is very important to be
active throughout life and especially when one gets older.

Music for Life Project, focus-group participants

Final word

Our overarching key messages are:

- Music-making is a joyful activity that brings with it many wider benefits. It may also function as a cost-effective and compassionate activity that mitigates many of the challenges of ageing, in particular loneliness, depression, loss of social networks, and living with the lost possible-selves of our earlier adult lives.
- Individuals at all stages of the lifecourse are entitled to fair and equitable access to high quality musical opportunities.
- Older people can and do develop musically. Musical development can occur across the lifespan, despite constraints associated with ageing.
- Older age can be a period of intense creativity where engagement in music-making can provide a vehicle for discovering a sense of coherence in one's life and for reaffirming and exploring major life themes.
- In order for the links between music-making, active ageing, and wellbeing to be strengthened, investment needs to be made in continuing professional development opportunities for teachers, facilitators, and care-givers.
- Policies and programmes that are concerned with participation in music amongst older people need to celebrate the prior experience that older people bring to their music-making, and should be responsive to the specific needs, capacities, and desires of the communities of older people they serve.
- Music-making for older people needs to be grounded within local communities, with opportunities for intergenerational collaboration and involvement of families and care-givers. Partnerships between music providers and community groups, assisted living, and residential care facilities are needed in order to serve older people in a range of settings.
- Opportunities for purposeful and meaningful performing and sharing of music-making within the community (including amongst people in residential care) can reinforce a sense of social affirmation amongst the music-makers, as well as strengthening links amongst generations.

As we prepare for old age and support our families, friends, and wider community members who have reached the Third and Fourth Ages, it is incumbent upon us all to listen and respond to the stories of older people who have experienced the benefits that music-making offers.

References

Age Concern (2008) *The Age Agenda 2008: Public policy and older people*. London: Age Concern.

Aldridge, F., and Tuckett, A. (2010) *A Change for the Better: The NIACE survey on adult participation in learning 2010*. Leicester: NIACE.

Allison, P.J., Locker, D., and Feine, J.S. (1997) 'Quality of life: A dynamic construct'. *Social Science & Medicine*, 45 (2), 221–30.

Allison, T.A. (2008) 'Songwriting and transcending institutional boundaries in the nursing home'. In Koen, B.D. (ed.) *The Oxford Handbook of Medical Ethnomusicology*. New York: Oxford University Press, 218–45.

Altenmüller, E.O. (2003) 'How many music centres are in the brain?' In Peretz, I. and Zatorre, R. (eds) *The Cognitive Neuroscience of Music*. Oxford: Oxford University Press, 346–56.

Altenmüller, E., Marco-Palleres, J., Münte, T.F., and Schneider, S. (2009) 'Neural reorganization underlies improvement in stroke-induced motor dysfunction by music-supported therapy'. *Annals of the New York Academy of Sciences,* 1169 (July), 395–405.

Amer, T., Kalender, B., Hasher, L., Trehub, S.E., and Wong, Y. (2013) 'Do older professional musicians have cognitive advantage?' *PLoS ONE*, 8 (8) e71630. Online. www.plosone.org/article/info:doi/10.1371/journal.pone.0071630 (accessed 6 September 2013).

Armstrong, F. (2012) 'Landscapes, spatial justice and learning communities'. *International Journal of Inclusive Education,* 16 (5/6), 609–26.

Ashley, M. (2002) 'Singing, gender and health: perspectives from boys singing in a church choir'. *Health Education,* 102 (4), 180–6.

Audit Commission (2008) *Don't Stop Me Now: Preparing for an ageing population. Local government national report*. London: Audit Commission. Online. www.cpa.org.uk/cpa/Dont_Stop_Me_Now.pdf (accessed 17 August 2013).

Baltes, P.B., and Baltes, M.M. (eds) (1990) *Successful Aging: Perspectives from the behavioral sciences*. New York: Cambridge University Press.

Baltes, P.B., Lindenberger, U., and Staudinger, U.M. (2006) 'Life-span theory in developmental psychology'. In Lerner, R.M. and Damon, W. (eds) *Handbook of Child Psychology, Volume One: Theoretical models of Human Development*. 6th ed. Hoboken, NJ: Wiley, 569–664.

Baltes, P.B., and Smith, J. (2003) 'New frontiers in the future of aging: From successful aging of the young old to the dilemmas of the fourth age'. *Gerontology,* 49 (2), 123–35.

Bamberger, J.S. (2006) 'What develops in musical development?' In Mcpherson, G.E. (ed.), *The Child as Musician*. Oxford: Oxford University Press, 69–92.

Baumgartner, H. (1992) 'Remembrance of things past: Music, autobiographical memory, and emotion'. *Cognition and Emotion*, 23, 1181–220.

Beck, R.J., Cesari, T.C., Yousefi, A., and Enamoto, H. (2000) 'Choral singing, performance perception, and immune system changes in salivary immunoglobulin A and cortisol'. *Music Perception*, 18 (1), 87–106.

Beck, R.J., Gottfried, T.L., Hall, D.J., Cisler, C.A., and Bozeman, K.W. (2006) 'Supporting the health of college solo singers: the relationship of positive emotions and stress to changes in salivary IgA and cortisol during singing'. *Journal of Learning through the Arts: A Research Journal on Arts Integration in Schools and Communities*, 2 (1), article 19.

Bekkouche, N.S., Holmes, S., Whittaker, K.S., and Krantz, D.S. (2011) 'Stress and the heart: Psychosocial stress and coronary heart disease'. In Contrada, R.J. and Baum, A. (eds) *The Handbook of Stress Science: Biology, psychology and health.* New York: Springer Publishing Co., 385–98.

Betts Adams, K., Leibbrandt, S., and Moon, H. (2011) 'A critical review of the literature on social and leisure activity and wellbeing in later life'. *Ageing and Society*, 31 (4), 683–712.

Bialystok, E., and DePape, A.M. (2009) 'Musical expertise, bilingualism, and executive functioning.' *Journal of Experimental Psychology, Human Perception and Performance*, 35 (2), 565–74.

Blacking, J. (1995) *Music, Culture, and Experience.* London: University of Chicago Press.

Blair, M.E., and Shimp, T.A. (1992) 'Consequences of an unpleasant experience with music: A second order negative conditioning perspective'. *Journal of Advertising,* 21, 35–43.

Bonde, L.O. (2011) 'Health music(k)ing: Music therapy or music and health? A model, eight empirical examples and some personal reflections'. *Music and Arts in Action: (special issue: Health promotion and wellness)*, 3 (2), 120–40.

Bonilha, A.G., Onofre, F., Vieira, M.L., Prado, M.Y.A., and Martinez, J.A.B. (2009) 'Effects of singing classes on pulmonary function and quality of life in COPD patients'. *International Journal of COPD*, 4 (1), 1–8.

Boone James, J., and Wink, P. (2006) *The Crown of Life: Dynamics of the early postretirement period (Annual Review of Gerontology and Geriatrics vol. 26).* New York: Springer Publishing Co.

Boudiny, K., and Mortelmans, D. (2011) 'A critical perspective: Towards a broader understanding of active ageing'. *Electronic Journal of Applied Psychology,* 7 (1), 8–14.

Boulton-Lewis, G.M. (2010) 'Education and learning for the elderly: Why, how, what'. *Educational Gerontology*, 36 (3), 213–28.

Brownie, S., and Horstmanshof, L. (2012) 'Creating the conditions for self-fulfilment for aged care residents'. *Nursing Ethics*, 19 (6), 777–86.

Brownley, K.A., McMurray, R.G., and Hackney, A.C. (1995) 'Effects of music on physiological and affective response to graded treadmill exercise in trained and untrained runners'. *International Journal of Psychophysiology*, 19 (3), 193–201.

Bruhn, H. (2002) 'Musical development of elderly people'. *Psychomusicology: A Journal of Research in Music Cognition*, 18 (1–2), 59–75.

Bugos J.A., Perlstein, W.M., McCrae, C.S., Brophy, T.S., and Bedenbaugh, P.H. (2007) 'Individualized piano instruction enhances executive functioning and working memory in older adults'. *Aging and Mental Health* 11 (4), 464–71.

Bungay, H., and Skingley, A. (2008) *The Silver Song Club Project: A formative evaluation.* Canterbury: Canterbury Christ Church University.

Byrgen, L.A., Konlaan, B.B., and Johnasson, W.E. (1996) 'Attendance at cultural events, reading books or periodicals, and making music or singing in a choir as determinants for survival: Swedish interview survey of living conditions'. *British Medical Journal,* 313 (7072), 1577–80.

Cacioppo, J.T., Berntson, G.G., Sheridan, J.F., and McClintock, M.K. (2000) 'Multilevel integrative analyses of human behavior: Social neuroscience and the complementing nature of social and biological approaches'. *Psychological Bulletin,* 126 (6), 829–43.

Calleo, J., and Stanley, M. (2008) 'Anxiety disorders in later life differentiated diagnosis and treatment strategies', *Psychiatric Times* 25 (8), 1–8. Online. http://topics.searchmedica.com/diabetes/content/article/10168/1166976 (accessed 6 September 2013).

Chang-Quan, H., Xue–Mei, Z., Bi-Rong, D., Zhen-Chan, L., Ji-Rong, Y., and Qing-Xiu, L. (2010) 'Health status and risk for depression among the elderly: A meta-analysis of published literature'. *Age and Ageing,* 39 (1), 23–30.

Charness, N. (1992) 'Age and expertise: Responding to Talland's challenge'. In I. W. Poon, I.W., Rubin, D.C., and Wilson, B.A. (eds) *Everyday Cognition in Adulthood and Later Life.* Cambridge, UK: Cambridge University Press, 437–56.

Clair, A. (1996) 'The effect of singing on alert responses in persons with late stage dementia'. *Journal of Music Therapy,* 33 (4), 234–47.

— (2000) 'The importance of singing with elderly patients'. In Aldridge, D. (ed.) *Music Therapy in Dementia Care.* London: Jessica Kingsley Publishers, 81–101.

Clark, F., Heller, A.F., Rafman, C., and Walker, J. (1997) 'Peer learning: A popular model for seniors education'. *Educational Gerontology,* 23 (8), 751–62.

Clift, S. (2012) 'Singing, wellbeing and health'. In MacDonald, R. Kreutz, G., and Mitchell, L. (eds) *Music, Health and Wellbeing.* Oxford: Oxford University Press, 111–24.

Clift, S., Hancox, G., Morrison, I., Hess, B., Kreutz, G., and Stewart, D. (2010) 'Choral singing and psychological wellbeing: Quantitative and qualitative findings from English choirs in a cross-national survey'. *Journal of Applied Arts and Health,* 1 (1), 19–34.

Clift, S., Hancox, G., Staricoff, R., and Whitmore, C. (2008) *Singing and Health: Summary of a systematic mapping; a review of non-clinical research,* Canterbury: Canterbury Christ Church University.

Clift, S., Skingley, A., Coulton, S., and Rodriguez, J. (2012) *A Controlled Evaluation of the Health Benefits of a Participative Community Singing Programme for Older People (Silver Song Clubs).* Canterbury: Sidney De Haan Research Centre for Arts and Health.

Coffman, D.D. (2002) 'Music and quality of life in older adults'. *Psychomusicology,* 18 (Spring–Summer), 76–88.

— (2009) 'Learning from our elders: Survey of new horizons international music association band and orchestra directors'. *International Journal of Community Music,* 2 (2/3), 227–40.

Coffman, D.D., and Adamek, M. (1999) 'The contribution of wind band participation to quality of life of senior adults'. *Music Therapy Perspectives,* 17 (1), 27–31.

— (2001) 'Perceived social support of new horizons band participants'. *Contributions to Music Education,* 28 (1), 27–40.

Coffman, D., and Levy, K. (1997) 'Senior adult bands: Music's new horizon'. *Music Educators Journal*, 84 (3), 17–22.

Cohen, A., Bailey, B., and Nilsson, T. (2002) 'The importance of music to seniors'. *Psychomusicology: A Journal of Research in Music Cognition*, 18 (0275–3987), 89–102.

Cohen, G. (2009) 'New theories and research findings on the positive influence of music and art on health with ageing'. *Arts & Health*, 1 (1), 48–62.

Cohen, G.D., Perlstein, S., Chapline, J., Kelly, J., Firth, K.M., and Simmens, S. (2006) 'The impact of professionally conducted cultural programs on the physical health, mental health, and social functioning of older adults'. *The Gerontologist*, 46 (6), 726–34.

— (2007) 'The impact of professionally conducted cultural programs on the physical health, mental health and social functioning of older adults: 2-year results'. *Journal of Aging, Humanities and the Arts*, 1 (1), 5–22.

Cohen, S., and Doyle, W. J. (1997) 'Social ties and susceptibility to the common cold'. *JAMA: Journal of the American Medical Association*, 277 (24), 1940–4.

Colcombe, S., and Kramer, A.F. (2003) 'Fitness effects on the cognitive function of older adults: A meta-analytic study'. *Psychological Science*, 14 (2), 125–30.

Conrad, C., Niess, H., Jauch, K.W., Bruns, C.J., Hartl, W., and Welker, L. (2007) 'Overture for growth hormone: requiem for interleukin–6?' *Critical Care Medicine*, 35 (12), 2709–13.

Conradson, D. (2003) 'Spaces of care in the city: The place of a community drop-in centre'. *Social & Cultural Geography*, 4 (4), 507–25.

Conway, C.M., and Hodgman, T. (2008) 'College and community choir member experiences in a collaborative intergenerational performance project'. *Journal of Research in Music Education*, 56 (3), 220–37.

Conway, C.M., Pisoni, D.B., and Kronenberger, W.G. (2009) 'The importance of sound for cognitive sequencing abilities: The auditory scaffolding hypothesis'. *Current Directions in Psychological Science*, 18 (5), 275–9.

Creech, A. (2012) 'Interpersonal behaviour in one to one instrumental lessons: An observational analysis'. *British Journal of Music Education*, 29 (3), 387–407.

Creech, A., Hallam, S., McQueen, H., and Varvarigou, M. (2013a) 'The power of music in the lives of older adults'. *Research Studies in Music Education*, 35 (1), 83–98.

Creech, A., Hallam, S., and Varvarigou, M. (2012) *Facilitating Music-Making for Older People: Facilitator's handbook – a continuing professional development resource for music leaders, facilitators and teachers*. London: Institute of Education, University of London, funded by the New Dynamics of Ageing Programme, Economic and Social Research Council. Online. www.soundsense. org/metadot/index.pl?id=27397 (accessed 17 August 2013).

Creech, A., Hallam, S., Varvarigou, M., McQueen, H., and Gaunt, H. (2013b) 'Active music making: A route to enhanced subjective well-being amongst older people'. *Perspectives in Public Health (Special Edition)*, 133 (1), 36–43.

Creech, A., Hallam, S., Varvarigou, M., McQueen, H., Gaunt, H., and Pincas, A. (2013c) 'The role of musical possible selves in supporting subjective well-being in later life'. *Music Education Research*, 16 (1) Online. http://tinyurl.com/ohncxjd (requires subscription).

Creech, A., and Long, M. (2012) *Self-directed and interdependent learning in musical contexts.* Proceedings of the Twenty-fourth International Seminar on Research in Music Education, Thessaloniki, Greece, 8–13 July.

Creech, A., Varvarigou, M., Hallam, S., McQueen, H., and Gaunt, H. (2013d) 'Scaffolding, organizational structure and interpersonal interaction in musical activities with older people'. *Psychology of Music,* Online. http://pom.sagepub.com/content/early/2013/03/12/0305735613478313.abstract (requires subscription).

Cross, I. (2009) 'The nature of music and its evolution'. In Hallam, S., Cross, I., and Thaut, M. (eds) *The Oxford Handbook of Music Psychology.* Oxford: Oxford University Press, 3–13.

Cross, S., and Markus, H. (1991) 'Possible selves across the life span'. *Human Development,* 34 (4), 230–55.

Cusicanqui, M., and Salmon, R. (2005) 'Seniors, small fry, and song: a group work libretto of an intergenerational singing group'. *Journal of Gerontological Social Work,* 44 (1–2), 189–210.

Daatland, S.O. (2005) 'Quality of life and ageing'. In Johnson, M.L. (ed.), *The Cambridge Handbook of Age and Ageing.* New York: Cambridge University Press, 371–7.

Dabback, W.M. (2005) 'Examining the gap between theory and emerging practices in the instrumental music education of older adults'. *International Journal of Community Music,* B (1), 1–16. Online. http://tinyurl.com/oqtflpw (accessed 27 August 2013).

— (2008a) 'Exploring social networks, reciprocity, and trust in a senior adult band'. Paper presented at the International Society for Music Education, 11th Community Music Activity International Seminar, Rome, Italy, 15–18 July. Online. http://tinyurl.com/q79elwv (accessed 23 August 2013).

— (2008b) 'Identity formation through participation in the Rochester New Horizons Band programme'. *International Journal of Community Music,* 1 (2), 267–86.

Dabback, W.M., and Smith, D.S. (2012) 'Elders and music: Empowering learning, valuing life experience, and considering the needs of aging adult learners'. In McPherson, G.E., and Welch, G. (eds) *The Oxford Handbook of Music Education* (Vol. 2). New York: Oxford University Press, 229–42.

Darkenwald, G.G., and Merriam, S.B. (1982) *Adult Education: Foundations of practice.* New York: Harper Row Publishers.

Darrough, G.P., and Boswell, J. (1992) 'Older adult participants in music: Making choral music with older adults'. *Music Educators Journal,* 79 (4), 27–9.

Darrow, A.A., and Belgrave, M. (2013) 'Students with Disabilities in intergenerational programmes'. *General Music Today,* 26 (2), 27–9.

Darrow, A.A., Johnson, C.M., and Ollenberger, T. (1994) 'The effect of participation in an intergenerational choir on teens' and older persons' cross-age attitudes'. *Journal of Music Therapy,* 31 (2), 119–34.

Darrow, A.A., Johnson, C., Ollenberger, T., and Miller, M.A. (2001) 'The Effect of an intergenerational choir performance on audience members' attitudinal statements towards teens and older persons'. *International Journal of Music Education,* 38 (1), 43–50.

Davidson, R.J., Scherer, K.R., and Goldsmith, H.H. (eds) (2003) *Handbook of Affective Sciences.* Oxford: Oxford University Press.

DeNora, T. (2000) *Music in Everyday Life*. Cambridge: Cambridge University Press.

— (2007) 'Health and music in everyday life – a theory of practice'. *Psyke & Logos,* 28 (1), 271–87.

Deci, E. L., and Ryan, R. M. (2000) 'The "what" and "why" of goal pursuits: Human needs and the self-determination of behavior'. *Psychological Inquiry*, 11 (4), 227–68.

— (2010) *Self-Determination Theory: An approach to human motivation & personality*. Online. www.psych.rochester.edu/SDT/ (accessed 7 September 2013).

Dench, S., and Regan, J. (2000) *Learning in Later Life: Motivation and impact*. Nottingham, UK: Department for Education and Employment.

Department of Health (2001) *The National Service Framework for Older People*. London: Department of Health.

Department of Work and Pensions (2005) *Opportunity Age: Meeting the challenges of ageing in the 21st century*. London: Department of Work and Pensions.

— (2008) *Opportunity Age Volume Two: A social portrait of ageing in the UK*. London: Department of Work and Pensions.

de Vries, P. (2012) 'Intergenerational music making: a phenomenological study of three older Australians making music with children'. *Journal of Research in Music Education,* 59 (4), 339–56.

Diefenbach, M.A., Miller, S.M., Porter, M., Peters, E., Stefanek, M., and Leventhal, H. (2008) 'Affect and screening for cancer: A self-regulation perspective'. In Lewis, M., Haviland-Jones, J.M., and Feldman Barrett, L. (eds) *Handbook of Emotion*. 3rd ed. New York: Guildford Press, 645–60.

Doyal, L., and Gough, I. (1991) *A Theory of Human Need*. Hong Kong: Macmillan.

Duay, D., and Bryan, V. (2008) 'Learning in later life: What seniors want in a learning experience'. *Educational Gerontology*, 34 (12), 1070–86.

Duke, R.A. (2000) 'Measures of instructional effectiveness in music research'. *Bulletin of the Council for Research in Music Education,* 143, 1–48.

Duke, R.A., Cash, C.D., and Allen, S.E. (2011) 'Focus of attention affects performance of motor skills in music'. *Journal of Research in Music Education*, 59 (1), 44–55.

Erikson, E. (1963) *Childhood and Society*. New York: W.W. Norton & Company Inc.

Ernst, R.E., and Emmons, S. (1992) 'New horizons for senior adults'. *Music Educators Journal*, 79 (4), 30–4.

Evers, S., and Suhr, B. (2000) 'Changes of the neurotransmitter serotonin but not of hormones during short term music perception'. *European Archives of Psychiatry and Clinical Neuroscience*, 250 (3), 144–7.

Fillit, H., Butler, R., O'Connell, A., Albert, M., Birren, J., Cotman, C., Greenough, W., Gold, P., Kramer, A., Kuller, L., Perls, T., Sahagan, B., and Tully, T. (2002) 'Achieving and maintaining cognitive vitality with aging'. *Mayo Clinic Proceedings*, 77 (7), 681–96.

Findsen, B. (2005) *Learning Later*. Malabar, Florida: Krieger Publishing Co.

Finnegan, R. (1989) *The Hidden Musicians: Music-making in an English town*. Cambridge: Cambridge University Press.

Fisher, B.J., and Specht, D.K. (1999) 'Successful aging and creativity in later life'. *Journal of Aging Studies*, 13 (4), 457–72.

Flowers, P.J., and Murphy, J.W. (2001) 'Talking about music: Interviews with older adults about their music education, preferences, activities, and reflections'. *Update: Applications of Research in Music Education*, 20 (1), 26–32.

Formosa, M. (2002) 'Critical gerogogy: Developing practical possibilities for critical educational gerontology'. *Education and Ageing*, 17 (1), 73–85.

— (2011) 'Critical educational gerontology: A third statement of first principles'. *International Journal of Education and Ageing*, 2 (1), 317–32.

Forssen, A.S.K. (2007) 'Humour, beauty, and culture as personal health resources: Experiences of elderly Swedish women'. *Scandinavian Journal of Public Health*, 35 (3), 228–34.

Foster and Partners (2013) *The Sage, Gateshead, UK*. Online. www.fosterandpartners.com/projects/the–sage–gateshead/ (accessed 1 September 2013).

Fowler, J.H., and Christakis, N.A. (2008) 'Dynamic spread of happiness in a large social network: Longitudinal analysis of the Framingham heart study social network'. *British Medical Journal*, 338 (7685), 23–31.

Fraser, H. (2006) *Evaluation of First Taste's Project: Melody, memory & movement*. Matlock, Derbyshire: First Taste.

Fraser, H. (2009) *Evaluation of First Taste's Project: Tutoring older people in care (TOPIC)*. Matlock, Derbyshire: First Taste.

Frazier, L., Johnson, P., Gonzalez, G., and Kafka, C. (2002) 'Psychosocial influences on possible selves: A comparison of three cohorts of older adults'. *International Journal of Behavioral Development*, 26 (4), 308–17.

Frego, D. (1995) 'Utilising the generations with music programmes'. *Music Educators Journal*, 81 (6), 17–19, 55.

Freire, P. (1970) *Pedagogy of the Oppressed*. London: Continuum.

Fries, J.F. (2012) 'The theory and practice of active aging'. *Current Gerontology and Geriatrics Research*, 2012 (420637), 1–7.

Fukui, H., and Yamashita, M. (2003) 'The effects of music and visual stress on testosterone and cortisol in men and women'. *Neuroendocrinology Letters*, 24 (3/4), 173–80.

Gagné, M. (2003) 'The role of autonomy support and autonomy orientation in prosocial behavior engagement'. *Motivation and Emotion*, 27 (3), 199–223.

Gallacher, J., Mitchell, C., Heslop, L., and Christopher, G. (2012) 'Resilience to health related adversity in older people'. *Quality in Ageing and Older Adults*, 13 (3), 197–204.

Garber, S. J. (2004) 'The Hand-in-Hand Community Music Programme: A case study'. Ph.D. diss., Australian National University, Canberra.

Gaser, C., and Schlaug, G. (2003) 'Brain structures differ between musicians and non-musicians'. *Journal of Neuroscience*, 23 (27), 9240–5.

Gembris, H. (2006) 'Research on musical development in a lifespan perspective – An introduction'. In Gembris, H. (ed.) *Musical Development from a Lifespan Perspective*, Frankfurt: Peter Lang, 11–20.

— (2008) 'Musical activities in the Third Age: An empirical study with amateur musicians'. In Daubney, A., Longhi, E., Lamont, A., and Hargreaves, D.J. (eds) *Musical Development and Learning*. Proceedings of the Second European Conference on Developmental Psychology of Music, Roehampton University, England, 10–12 September. Hull: G.K. Publishing, 103–8.

— (2012) 'Music-making as a lifelong development and resource for health'. In MacDonald, R., Kreutz, G., and Mitchell, L. (eds) *Music, Health, and Wellbeing* (Kindle Edition, Chapter 25). Oxford: Oxford University Press.

George, L. (2005) 'Stress and coping'. In Johnson, M.L. (ed.) *The Cambridge Handbook of Age and Ageing.* New York: Cambridge University Press, 292–300.

Gerra, G., Zaimovic, A., Franchini, D., Palladino, M., Giucastro, G., Reali, N., Maestri, D., Caccavari, R., Delsignore, R., and Brambilla, F. (1998) 'Neuroendocrine responses of healthy volunteers to "techno-music": relationships with personality trait and emotional state'. *International Journal of Psychophysiology,* 28 (1), 99–111.

Gibbons, A.C. (1982) 'Music aptitude profile scores in a non-institutionalized, elderly population'. *Journal of Research in Music Education,* 30 (1), 23–9.

— (1983). 'Musical skill level self-evaluation in non-institutionalized elderly'. *Activities, Adaptation and Aging,* 3 (2), 61–67.

— (1985) 'Stop babying the elderly'. *Music Educators Journal,* 71 (7), 48–51.

Gifford, R. (1997) *Environmental Psychology: Principles and practice.* 2nd ed. Boston: Allyn & Bacon.

Glendenning, F. (ed.). (2000) *Teaching and Learning in Later Life.* Aldershot, England: Ashgate.

Glendenning, F., and Battersby, D. (1990) 'Why we need educational gerontology and education for older adults: A statement of first principles'. In Glendenning, F. and Percy, K. (eds) *Ageing, Education and Society: Readings in educational gerontology,* The University, Keele: Association for Educational Gerontology, 219–31.

Goff, K. (1992) 'Enhancing creativity in older adults'. *Journal of Creative Behavior,* 26 (1), 40–9.

Goolsby T.W. (1994) 'Profiles of processing: Eye movements during sightreading'. *Music Perception* 12 (1), 97–123.

Gordon, F. (1965) *Musical Aptitude Profile.* Boston: Houghton Mifflin.

GOScience (2008) *Foresight Mental Capital and Well-Being Project.* London: The Government Office for Science.

Grape, C., Sandgren, M., Hansson, L.O., Ericson, M., and Theorell, T. (2003) 'Does singing promote well–being? An empirical study of professional and amateur singers during a singing lesson'. *Integrative Physiological and Behavioural Science,* 38 (1), 65–74.

Green, L. (2008) *Music, Informal Learning and the School: A new classroom pedagogy.* Aldershot: Ashgate Publishers.

Greenwald, M.A., and Salzberg, R S. (1979) 'Vocal range assessment of geriatric clients'. *Journal of Music Therapy,* 16 (4), 172–9.

Gruenewald, D.A. (2008) 'The best of both worlds: A critical pedagogy of place'. *Environmental Education Research,* 14 (3), 308–24.

Hagen, E.H., and Bryant, G.A. (2003) 'Music and dance as a coalition signaling system'. *Human Nature,* 14 (1), 21–51.

Hallam, S. (1998) *Instrumental Teaching.* Oxford: Heinemann.

— (2001) *The Power of Music: The strength of music influence on our lives.* London: The Performing Rights Society UK.

— (2005) *Enhancing Motivation and Learning Throughout the Lifespan.* London: Institute of Education, University of London.

— (2006a) 'Musicality'. In McPherson, G.E. (ed.) *The Child as Musician*. Oxford: Oxford University Press, 93–110.

— (2006b) *Music Psychology in Education*. London: Institute of Education, University of London.

— (2010) 'The power of music: its impact on the intellectual, social and personal development of children and young people'. *International Journal of Music Education*, 28 (3), 269–89.

Hallam, S., Creech, A., Gaunt, H., Pincas, A., McQueen, H., and Varvarigou, M. (2011) *Music for Life Project: Promoting social engagement and well-being through community supported participation in musical activities: Final report.* London: Institute of Education, University of London and Guildhall School of Music & Drama, funded by the ESRC New Dynamics of Ageing Programme.

Hallam, S., Creech, A., Gaunt, H., Pincas, A., Varvarigou, M., and McQueen, H. (2013) 'Does active engagement in community music promote enhanced quality of life in older people?' *Arts & Health*. Online. www.tandfonline.com/doi/full/10.1080/17533015.2013.809369#.Uwue0GKEMVA (requires subscription).

Hallam, S., Creech, A., Varvarigou, M., and McQueen, H. (2012) 'Perceived benefits of active engagement with making music in community settings'. *International Journal of Community Music*, 5 (2), 155–74.

Hallam, S., Rogers, L., and Creech, A. (2008) 'Gender differences in musical instrument choice', *International Journal of Music Education*, 26 (1), 7–19.

Hanna-Pladdy, B., and Gajewski, B. (2012) 'Recent and past musical activity predicts cognitive aging variability: direct comparison with general lifestyle activities'. *Frontiers in Human Neuroscience*, 6 (198). Online. www.frontiersin.org/Human_Neuroscience/10.3389/fnhum.2012.00198/full (accessed 6 September 2013).

Hanna-Pladdy B., and MacKay, A. (2011) 'The relation between instrumental musical activity and cognitive aging'. *Neuropsychology* 25 (3), 378–86.

Hargreaves, D., and North, A. (eds) (1997) *The Social Psychology of Music*. Oxford: Oxford University Press.

Harrer, G., and Harrer, H. (1977) 'Music, emotion and autonomic function'. In M. Critchley, M. and Henson, R.A. (eds) *Music and the Brain: Studies in the neurology of music*. London: William Heinemann, 202–16.

Hasher, L., Zacks, R.T., and May, C.P. (1999) 'Inhibitory control, circadian arousal, and age'. In Gopher, D. and Koriat, A. (eds) *Attention and Performance, XVII, Cognitive Regulation of Performance: Interaction of theory and application.* Cambridge, MA: MIT Press, 653–75.

Hatton-Yeo, A. (2006) *Intergenerational Programmes: An introduction and examples of practice*. Stoke-on-Trent: Beth Johnson Foundation. Online. http://tinyurl.com/qfcj4xw (accessed 6 September 2013).

Hays, T., and Minichiello, V. (2005) 'The contribution of music to quality of life in older people: An Australian qualitative study'. *Ageing & Society*, 25 (2), 261–78.

Heckhausen, J., Wrosch, C., and Schulz, R. (2010) 'A motivational theory of life-span development'. *Psychological Review*, 117 (1), 32–60.

Heenan, D. (2011) 'How local interventions can build capacity to address social isolation in dispersed rural communities: A case study from Northern Ireland.' *Ageing International*, 36 (4), 475–91.

Heron, J. (1999) *The Complete Facilitator's Handbook*. London: Kogan Page Ltd.

Herrmann, S., Sipsas-Herrmann, A., Stafford, M., and Herrmann, N. (2006) 'Benefits and risks of intergenerational program participation by senior citizens'. *Educational Gerontology*, 31 (2), 123–38.

Hickson, J., and Housley, W. (1997) 'Creativity in later life'. *Educational Gerontology*, 23 (6), 539–47.

Hiemstra, R. (1991) 'Aspects of Effective Learning Environments'. *New Directions for Adult and Continuing Education*, 1991 (50), 5–12.

Higgs, P., Hyde, M., Wiggins, R., and Blane, D. (2003) 'Researching quality of life in early old age: The importance of the sociological dimension'. *Social Policy & Administration*, 37 (3), 239–52.

Hillman, S. (2002) 'Participatory singing for older people: A perception of benefit'. *Health Education*, 102 (4), 163–71.

Hodge, J. (1990) 'The quality of life: A contrast between utilitarian and existentialist approaches'. In Baldwin, S., Godfrey, C., and Propper, G. (eds) *Quality of Life: Perspectives and policies*. London: Routledge, 42–57.

Hornquist, J.O. (1990) 'Quality of life'. *Scandinavian Journal of Public Health*, 18 (1), 69–79.

Houston, D.M., McKee, K.J., Carroll, L., and Marsh, H. (1998) 'Using humour to promote psychological wellbeing in residential homes for older people'. *Aging and Mental Health*, 2 (4), 328–32.

Hulme, C., Wright, J., Crocker, T., Oluboyede, Y., and House, A. (2008) *A Systematic Review of Non-Drug Treatments for Dementia*. Leeds: Leeds Institute of Health Sciences, Faculty of Medicine and Health, University of Leeds.

Huron, D. (2003) 'Is music an evolutionary adaptation?' In Peretz, I. and Zatorre, R. (eds) *The Cognitive Neuroscience of Music*. Oxford: Oxford University Press, 57–77.

Hyde, K.L., Lerch, J., Norton, A., Forgeard, M., Winner, E., Evans, A.C., and Schlaug, G. (2009) 'Musical training shapes structural brain development'. *Journal of Neuroscience*, 29 (10), 3019–25.

Hyde, M.M., Wiggins, R.D., Higgs, P.P., and Blane, D.B. (2003) 'A measure of quality of life in early old age: The theory, development and properties of a needs satisfaction model (CASP–19)'. *Ageing & Mental Health*, 7 (3), 186–94.

Ibarra, H. (1999) 'Provisional selves: Experimenting with image and identity in professional adaptation'. *Administrative Science Quarterly*, 44 (4), 764–91.

Jacobi, M., and Stokols, D. (1983) 'The role of tradition in group-environment relations'. In Feimer, N.R. and Geller, E.S. (eds) *Environmental Psychology: Directions and perspectives*. New York: Praeger Press, 157–79.

Jansen, D.A. (2005) 'Perceived barriers to participation in mentally restorative activities by community-dwelling elders'. *Activities, Adaptation & Aging*, 29 (2), 35–53.

Jansen, D.A., and von Sadovszky, V. (2004) 'Restorative activities of community dwelling elders'. *Western Journal of Nursing Research*, 26 (4), 381–99.

Jenkins, A. (2011) 'Participation in learning and wellbeing among older adults'. *International Journal of Lifelong Education*, 30 (3), 403–20.

Jenkins, A., and Mostafa, T. (2012) *Learning and Wellbeing Trajectories Among Older Adults in England*. (BIS Research Paper Number 92). Institute of Education, University of London: Department for Business, Innovation & Skills.

JISC (2006) *Designing Spaces for Effective Learning: A guide to 21st century learning space design*. Bristol: JISC. Online. www.jisc.ac.uk/uploaded_documents/JISClearningspaces.pdf (accessed 1 September 2013).

Johnston, M.M., and Finney, S.J. (2010) 'Measuring basic needs satisfaction: Evaluating previous research and conducting new psychometric evaluations of the basic needs satisfaction in general scale'. *Contemporary Educational Psychology*, 35, 280–96.

Jones, G.G. (2005) *Midwives and Fellow Travellers: The craft and artistry of adult educators*. London: Mary Ward Centre.

Juslin, P.N., Liljestrom, S., Laukka, P., Vastfjall, D., and Lundqvist, L.O. (2011) 'Emotional reactions to music in a nationally representative sample of Swedish adults: Prevalence and causal influences'. *Musicae Scientiae*, 15, 174–207.

Juslin, P.N., Liljestrom, S., Vastfjall, D., and Lundqvist, L.O. (2010) 'How does music evoke emotions? Exploring the underlying mechanisms'. In Juslin, P.N. and Sloboda, J.A. (eds) *Handbook of Music and Emotion: Theory, research, applications*. Oxford: Oxford University Press, 605–42.

Juslin, P.N., and Sloboda, J.A. (eds) (2010) *Handbook of Music and Emotion: Theory, research, applications*. Oxford: Oxford University Press.

Jutras, P.J. (2006) 'The benefits of adult piano tuition as self-reported by selected adult piano students'. *Journal of Research in Music Education*, 54 (2), 97–110.

Kalache, A., Farreto, S.M., and Keller, I. (2005) 'Global ageing: The demographic revolution in all cultures and societies'. In Johnson, M. (ed.) *The Cambridge Handbook of Age and Ageing*. Cambridge: Cambridge University Press, 30–46.

Kalakoski, V. (2007) 'Effect of skill level on recall of visually presented patterns of musical notes'. *Scandanavian Journal of Psychology*, 48 (2), 87–96.

Kamin, S., Richards, H., and Collins, D. (2007) 'Influences on the talent development process of non-classical musicians: Psychological, social and environmental influences'. *Music Education Research*, 9 (3), 449–68.

Keaney, E., and Oskala, A. (2007) 'The golden age of the arts? Taking part survey findings on older people and the arts'. *Cultural Trends*, 16 (4), 323–55.

Keitz, M., Martin-Soelch, C., and Leenders, K.L. (2003) 'Reward processing in the brain: A prerequisite for movement preparation?' *Neural Plasticity*, 10 (1–2), 121–8.

Kerschner, H., and Pegues, J. M. (1998) 'Productive aging: A quality of life agenda'. *Journal of the American Dietetic Association*, 98 (12), 1445–8.

King, L.A., and Hicks, J.A. (2007) 'Whatever happened to "what might have been"? Regrets, happiness, and maturity'. *American Psychologist*, 62 (7), 625–36.

Kline, D.W., and Scialfa, C.T. (1996) 'Visual and auditory ageing'. In Birren, J.E., and Schaie, K.W. (eds), *Handbook of the Psychology of Ageing*. 4th ed. 181–203. San Diego: Academic Press.

Kotter-Grühn, D., and Smith, J. (2011) 'When time is running out: Changes in positive future perception and their relationships to changes in well-being in old age'. *Psychology and Aging*, 26 (2), 381–7.

Krampe, R.T. (1994) *Maintaining Excellence: Cognitive motor performance in pianists differing in age and skill level*. Berlin: Max Planck Institut fur Bildung und Forschung.

— (2006) 'Musical expertise from a life-span perspective'. In Gembris, H. (ed.) *Musical Development from a Lifespan Perspective*. Frankfurt: Peter Lang, 91–106.

Krampe, R.T., and Ericsson, K.A. (1996) 'Maintaining excellence: Deliberate practice and elite performance in young and older pianists'. *Journal of Experimental Psychology: General*, 125 (4), 331–59.

Kreutz, G., Bongard, S., Rohrmann, S., Hodapp, V., and Grebe, D. (2004) 'Effects of choir singing or listening on secretory immunoglobulin A, cortisol and emotional state'. *Journal of Behavioural Medicine*, 27, 623–34.

Kreutz, G., and Lotze, M. (2008) 'Neuroscience of music and emotion'. In Gruhn, W. and Rauscher, R. (eds) *The Neuroscience of Music Education*. New York: Nova Publishers, 145–69.

Kreutz, G., Murcia, C.Q., and Bongard, S. (2012) 'Psychoneuroendocrine Research on Music and Health: An overview'. In MacDonald, R., Kreuz, G., and L. Mitchell, L. (eds) *Music, Health and Wellbeing*. Oxford: Oxford University Press, 457–76.

Kubzansky, L.D. (2009) 'Health and emotion'. In Sander, D. and Scherer, K.R. (eds) *Oxford Companion to Emotion and the Affective Sciences*. Oxford: Oxford University Press, 204–5.

Kuh, G.D., Kinzie, J., Schuh, J.H., Whitt, E.J., and associates (2005) *Student Success in College: Creating conditions that matter*. San Fransisco: Jossey Bass.

Kuhn, D. (2002) 'The effects of active and passive participation in musical activity on the immune system as measured by salivary immunoglobulin A (SIgA)'. *Journal of Music Therapy*, 39 (1), 30–9.

Kumar, A.M., Tims, F., Cruess, D.G., Mintzer, M.J., Ironson, G., Loewenstein, D., Cattan, R., Fernandez, J.B., Eisdorfer, C., and Kumar, M. (1999) 'Music Therapy increases Serum Melatonin levels in patients with Alzheimer's disease'. *Alternative Therapies*, 5 (6), 49–57.

Lafortune, G., and Balestat, G. (2007) *Trends in Severe Disability Among Elderly People: Assessing the evidence in 12 OECD countries and the future implications (OECD Health Working Papers No 26)*. Paris: Organisation for Economic Co-operation and Development: Directorate for employment, labour and social affairs, health committee.

LaGasse, A.B., and Thaut, M.H. (2012) 'Music and Rehabilitation: Neurological Approaches'. In MacDonald, R., Kreutz, G., and Mitchell, L. (eds) *Music, Health and Wellbeing*. Oxford: Oxford University Press, 153–63.

Lally, E. (2009) 'The power to heal us with a smile and a song: Senior well-being, music-based participatory arts and the value of qualitative evidence'. *Journal of Arts and Communities*, 1 (1), 25–44.

La Marca, S. (2010) *Designing the Learning Environment: Learning in a changing world*. Victoria, Australia: ACER Press.

Lang, F.R., and Heckhausen, J. (2001) 'Perceived control over development and subjective well-being: Differential benefits across adulthood'. *Journal of Personality and Social Psychology*, 81 (3), 509–23.

Langston, T.W. (2011) 'It is a life support isn't it? Social capital in a community choir'. *International Journal of Community Music*, 4 (2), 163–84.

Langston, T.W., and Barrett, M.S. (2008) 'Capitalizing on community music: A case study of the manifestation of social capital in a community choir'. *Research Studies in Music Education,* 30 (2), 118–38.

Laslett, P. (1989) *A Fresh Map of Life: The emergence of the Third Age.* London: Weidenfeld and Nicholson.

Laukka, P. (2007) 'Uses of music and psychological well-being among the elderly'. *Journal of Happiness Studies,* 8 (2), 215–41.

Lehmberg, L.J., and Fung, V.C. (2010) 'Benefits of music participation for senior citizens: A review of the literature'. *Music Education Research International,* 4, 19–30.

Leondari, A., Syngollitu, E., and Kiosseoglou, G. (1998) 'Brief report: Academic achievement, motivation, and possible selves'. *Journal of Adolescence,* 21 (2), 219–22.

Le Roux, F.H., Bouic, P.J.D., and Bester, M.M. (2007) 'The effect of Bach's Magnificat on emotions, immune, and endocrine parameters during physiotherapy treatment of patients with infectious lung conditions', *Journal of Music Therapy,* 44 (2), 156–68.

Leventhal, H., and Patrick-Miller, L. (2000) 'Emotions and physical illness: Causes and indicators of vulnerability'. In Lewis, M., and Haviland-Jones, J.M. (eds) *Handbook of Emotions.* 2nd ed. New York: Guilford Press, 645–60.

Lewin, K., Lippit, R., and White, R.K. (1939) 'Patterns of aggressive behavior in experimentally created social climates'. *Journal of Social Psychology,* 10, 271–301.

Lim, F.V., Halloran, K.L., and Podlasov, A. (2012) 'Spatial pedagogy: Mapping meanings in the use of classroom space'. *Cambridge Journal of Education,* 42 (2), 235–51.

Litwin, H., and Shiovitz-Ezra, S. (2011) 'Social network type and subjective well-being in a national sample of older Americans'. *Gerontologist,* 51 (3), 379–88.

Lord, V.M., Cave, P., Hume, V., Flude, E.J., Evans, A., Kelly J.L., Polkey, M.I., and Hopkinson, N.S. (2010) 'Singing teaching as a therapy for chronic respiratory disease: a randomized controlled trial and qualitative evaluation'. *BMC Pulmonary Medicine,* 10 (41). Online. www.biomedcentral.com/1471–2466/10/41 (accessed 6 September 2013).

Lundqvist, L.O., Carlsson, F., Hilmersson, P., and Juslin, P.N. (2009) 'Emotional responses to music: Experience, expression and physiology', *Psychology of Music,* 37 (1), 61–90.

Macdonald, R., Miell, D., and Hargreaves, D. (eds) (2002) *Musical Identities.* Oxford: Oxford University Press.

Manheimer, R. J. (2009) 'Creating meaningful senior-friendly spaces'. *Generations,* 33 (2), 60–5.

Markus, H., and Nurius, P. (1986) 'Possible selves'. *American Psychologist,* 41 (9), 954–69.

Martinez, E. (2000) *Regência Coral – Princípios Básicos.* Curitiba: Dom Bosco.

Maslow, A. (1954) *Motivation and Personality.* New York: Harper & Row.

McCraty, R., Atkinson, M., Rein, G., and Watkins, A.D. (1996) 'Music enhances the effect of positive emotional states on salivary IgA'. *Stress Medicine,* 12, 167–75.

McKenna, S.P., Doward, L.C., Alonso, J., Kohlmann, T., Niero, M., Prieto, L., and Wiren, L. (1999) 'The qol-aghda: An instrument for the assessment of quality of life in adults with growth hormone deficiency'. *Quality of Life Research*, 8 (4), 373–83.

McKinney, C.H., Tims, F.C., Kumar, A.M., and Kumar, M. (1997) 'The effect of selected classical music and spontaneous imagery on Plasma B-Endorphin'. *Journal of Behavoural Medicine*, 20 (1), 85–99.

McNeill, W.H. (1995) *Keeping Together in Time: Dance and drill in human history.* Cambridge, MA: Harvard University Press.

McPherson, G.E. (1995/6) 'Five aspects of musical performance and their correlates'. *Bulletin of the Council for Research in Music Education*, 127 (Winter, special issue) 15th International Society for Music Education, Research Seminar, 9–15 July, University of Miami, Florida, 115–21.

McQueen, H., Hallam, S., Creech, A., and Varvarigou, M. (2013) 'A philosophical perspective on leading music activities for the over 50s'. *International Journal of Lifelong Education*, 32 (3), 353–77.

Mehrotra, C. (2011) 'In defence of offering educational programs for older adults'. *Educational Gerontology*, 29 (8), 645–55.

Meshel, D., and McGlynn, R. (2010) 'Intergenerational contact, attitudes, and stereotypes of adolescents and older people'. *Educational Gerontology*, 30 (6), 457–79.

Meyer, L.B. (1956) *Emotion and Meaning in Music.* Chicago: Chicago University Press.

Mitchell, L.A., and MacDonald, R.A.R. (2006) 'An experimental investigation of the effects of preferred music, arithmetic and humour on cold pressor pain'. *European Journal of Pain*, 10 (4), 343–51.

Möckel, M., Röcker, L., Störk, T., Vollert, J., Danne, O., Eichstädt, H., Müller, R., Hochrein, H. (1994) 'Immediate physiological responses of healthy volunteers to different types of music: cardiovascular, hormonal and mental changes'. *European Journal of Applied Physiology*, 68 (6), 451–9.

Morrison, I., and Clift, S. (2012a) *Singing and People with Chronic Obstructive Pulmonary Disease.* Canterbury: Canterbury Christ Church University.

— (2012b) *Singing and Mental Health.* Canterbury: Canterbury Christ Church University.

Moser, S.R. (2003) 'Beyond the Mozart effect: Age-related cognitive functioning in instrumental music participants'. *Dissertation Abstracts International Section A: Humanities and Social Sciences*, 64 (3–A), 760. Online. http://aquila.usm.edu/theses_dissertations/2333 (accessed 6 September 2013).

Motte, E. de la (2004), 'Giving and Receiving'. *Dandenong Ranges Music Council (2004), Annual Report*, 28–9.

Münte T.F., Altenmüller E., and Jäncke, L. (2002) 'The musician's brain as a model of neuroplasticity'. *National Review of Neuroscience*, 3 (6), 473–8.

Murcia, C.Q., Bongard, S., and Kreutz, G. (2009) 'Emotional and neurohumoral responses to dancing tango Argentine: The effects of music and partner'. *Music and Medicine*, 1 (1), 14–21.

Musica, Music and Wellbeing (2013) Online. http://musica–music.co.uk/ (accessed 25 July 2013).

Myers, D. (1988) 'Aging effects and older adult learners: Implications of an instructional program in music'. *Transactions of the Wisconsin Academy of Science, Arts, and Letters,* 76, 81–9.

— (1995) 'Lifelong learning: An emerging research agenda for music education'. *Research Studies in Music Education,* 4 (1, June), 21–6.

Myskyja, A. and Nord, P.G. (2008) 'The day the music died': A pilot study on music and depression in a nursing home. *Nordic Journal of Music Therapy,* 17 (1), 30–40.

Naughton, C., Bennett, K., and Feely, J. (2006) 'Prevalence of chronic disease in the elderly based on a national pharmacy claims database'. *Age and Ageing,* 35 (6), 633–6.

NDA (2013) *New Dynamics of Ageing Programme.* Online. www.newdynamics. group.shef.ac.uk/ (accessed 7 September 2013).

Neary, M., Harrison, A., Crellin, G., Parekh, N., Saunders, G., Duggan, F., Williams, S. and Austin, S. (2010) *Learning Landscapes in Higher Education (Report).* Lincoln: Centre for Educational Research and Development.

Nelson, A., Hartl, W Jauch, K-W., Fricchione, G.L., Benson, H., Warshaw, A.L., and Conrad, C. (2008) 'The impact of music on hypermetabolism in critical illness'. *Current Opinion in Clinical Nutrition and Metabolic Care,* 11 (6), 790–4.

Newman, S. and Hatton-Yeo, A. (2008) 'Intergenerational learning and the contribution of older people'. *Ageing Horizons,* 8 (2), 31–9.

Newman, S., Ward, C., Smith, T., Wilson, J., and McCrea, J. (1997) *Intergenerational Programmes: Past, present and future.* Washington DC: Taylor & Francis.

North, A.C., and Hargreaves, D.J. (2008) *The Social and Applied Psychology of Music.* Oxford: Oxford University Press.

Oblinger, D.G. (ed.) (2006) *Designing Spaces for Effective Learning: A guide to 21st century learning space.* Online. www.educause.edu/learningspaces (accessed 1 September 2013).

O'Connor, D.W., Ames, D., Gardner, B., and King, M. (2009a) 'Psychosocial treatments of behaviour symptoms in dementia: a systematic review of reports meeting quality standards'. *International Psychogeriatrics,* 21 (2), 225–40.

— (2009b) 'Psychosocial treatments for psychological symptoms in dementia: a systematic review of reports meeting quality standards'. *International Psychogeriatrics,* 21 (2), 241–51.

O'Neill, S., and Heydon, R. (2013) 'Elders connecting to young people through singing: Evidence of generativity and well-being among older adults in an intergenerational program'. Paper presented at the Advancing Interdisciplinary Research in Singing, Ryerson University, Toronto, 11–13 August.

ONS (2010) *Standard Occupational Classification 2010.* Office for National Statistics, UK. Online. www.ons.gov.uk/ons/guide–method/classifications/current–standard–classifications/soc2010/index.html (accessed 7 September 2013).

Osborne, J.W. (1981) 'The mapping of thoughts, emotions, sensations, and images as responses to music'. *Journal of Mental Imagery,* 5 (Spring), 133–6.

O'Shea, H. (2012) 'Get back to where you once belonged! The positive creative impact of a refresher course for baby-boomer rock musicians'. *Popular Music,* 31 (2), 199–215.

Palmer C., and Drake C. (1997) 'Monitoring and planning capacities in the acquisition of music performance skills'. *Canadian Journal of Experimental Psychology*, 51 (4), 369–84.

Panksepp, J., and Bernatzky, G. (2002) 'Emotional sounds and the brain: the neuro-affective foundations of musical appreciation'. *Behavioural Processes*, 60 (2), 133–55.

Pappas, J.P. (1990) 'Environmental psychology of the learning sanctuary'. *New Directions for Adult and Continuing Education*, 46, 41–52.

Parbery-Clark, A., Skoe, E., Lam, C., and Kraus, N. (2009) 'Musician enhancement for speech-in-noise.' *Ear and Hearing*, 3 (6), 653–61.

Parbery-Clark, A., Strait, D.L., Anderson, S., Hittner, E., and Kraus, N. (2011) 'Musical experience and the aging auditory system: Implications for cognitive abilities and hearing speech in noise'. *PLoS One*, 6 (5) e18082.

Patrick, H., Ryan, A.M., Alfred-Liro, C., Fredricks, J.A., Hruda, L.Z., and Eccles, J.S. (1999) 'Adolescents' commitment to developing talent: The role of peers in continuing motivation for sports and the arts'. *Journal of Youth and Adolescence*, 28 (6), 741–63.

Paúl, C., Ribeiro, O., and Teixeira, L. (2012) 'Active ageing: An empirical approach to the WHO model'. *Current Gerontology & Geriatrics Research*, 382972, 1–10.

Pavlicevic, M. (2012) 'Between beats: Group music therapy transforming people and places'. In MacDonald, R., Kreutz, G. and Mitchell, L. (eds) *Music Health and Wellbeing*. Oxford: Oxford University Press, 196–212.

Pelletier, K.R. (1992) 'Mind-Body Health: Research, Clinical, and Policy Applications'. *American Journal of Health Promotion*: 6 (5) May/June, 345–58.

Penhune, V. (2011) 'Sensitive periods in human development: Evidence from musical training'. *Cortex*, 47 (9), 1126–37.

Perez, I., and Zatorre, R.J. (2005) 'Brain organization for music processing'. *Annual Review of Psychology*, 56, 89–114.

Pike, P. (2011) 'Using technology to engage third-age (retired) leisure learners: A case study of a third-age MIDI piano ensemble'. *International Journal of Music Education*, 29 (2), 116–23.

Pilon, M.A., McIntosh, K.W., and Thaut, M.H. (1998) 'Auditory versus visual speech timing cues as external rate control to enhance verbal intelligibility in mixed spastic-ataxic dysarthric speakers: A pilot study'. *Brain Injury*, 12 (9), 793–803.

Pinker, S. (1997) *How the Mind Works*. New York: Norton.

Prickett, C. (2003) 'Is there musical life after graduation? Mining the resources of an understudied population'. *Research Studies in Music Education*, 21, 58–71.

Rogers, R. (2005) *Routes into Teaching Music: A guide for every kind of musician about how to train and work as a teacher of music*. London: DfES with Esmée Fairbairn Foundation.

Rossiter, M. (2007) 'Possible selves: An adult education perspective'. *New Directions for Adult & Continuing Education*, 2007 (114), 5–15.

RRA (2010) *The Relatives and Residents Association. News release: 40,000 older people in care 'isolated'*. Online. www.relres.org/images/RRA_Nov_2010%20_Isolation.pdf (accessed 31 December 2012).

Rubinstein, R.L. (2002) 'The Third Age'. In Weiss, R.S. and Bass, S.A. (eds) *Challenges of the Third Age: Meaning and purpose in later life*. New York: Oxford University Press, 29–40.

Saarikallio, S. (2011) 'Music as emotional self-regulation throughout adulthood'. *Psychology of Music*, 39 (3), 307–27.

Sage Gateshead (2013) *The Building*. Online. www.sagegateshead.com/about–us/where–we–do–it/the–building/ (accessed 1 September 2013).

Sandgren, M. (2009) 'Evidence of strong immediate well-being effects of choral singing – with more enjoyment for women than for men'. Paper presented at the 7th Triennial Conference of European Society for the Cognitive Sciences of Music (ESCOM 2009), Jyväskylä, Finland. August 12–16.

Scase, R., and Scales, J. (2000) *Fit and Fifty?* Swindon: Report prepared for the Economic and Social Research Council. Online. www.education.edean.org/pdf/Intro007.pdf (accessed 17 August 2013).

Schellenberg, E.G., and Moreno, S. (2010) 'Music lessons, pitch processing, and g'. *Psychology of Music*, 38 (2), 209–21.

Schindler, I., Staudinger, U., and Nesselroade, J. (2006) 'Development and structural dynamics of personal life investment in old age'. *Psychology and Ageing*, 21 (4), 737–53.

Schneider, K. (2011) 'The significance of learning for aging'. *Educational Gerontology*, 29 (10), 809–23.

Schneider P., Scherg, M., Dosch, H.G., Specht, H.J., Gutschalk, A., and Rupp, A. (2002) 'Morphology of Heschl's gyrus reflects enhanced activation in the auditory cortex of musicians'. *Nature Neuroscience*, 5 (7), 688–94.

Schneider, S., Schonle, P.W., Altenmüller, E., and Münte, T.F. (2007) 'Using musical instruments to improve motor skill recovery following a stroke', *Journal of Neurology*, 254 (10), 1339–46.

Schorr-Lesnick, B., Teirstein, A.S., Brown, L.K., and Miller, A. (1985) 'Pulmonary function in singers and wind-instrument players'. *Chest*, 88 (2), 201–5.

Schuller, T., and Watson, D. (2009) *Learning Through Life: Inquiry into the future for lifelong learning*. Leicester: NIACE.

Scourfield, P. (2007) 'Helping older people in residential care remain full citizens'. *British Journal of Social Work*, 37 (7), 1135–52.

Seltzer. J.A., and Yahirun, J.J. (2013) *Diversity in Old Age: The elderly in changing economic and family contexts*. Los Angeles: University of California.

Setterson, R.A. (2002) 'Social sources of meaning in later life'. In Weiss, R.S., and Bass, S.A. (eds) *Challenges of the Third Age: Meaning and purpose in later life*. New York: Oxford University Press, 55–80.

Simone, P.M., and Haas, A.L. (2013) 'Frailty, leisure activity and functional status in older adults: Relationship with subjective well being'. *Clinical Gerontologist*, 36 (4), 275–93.

Skingley, A., and Vella-Burrows, T. (2010) 'Therapeutic effects of music and singing for older people', *Nursing Standard*, 24 (19), 35–41.

Sluming, V., Barrick, T., Howard, M., Cezayirli, E., Mayes, A., and Roberts, N. (2002) 'Voxel-based morphometry reveals increased gray matter density in Broca's area in male symphony orchestra musicians'. *Neuroimage*, 17 (3), 1613–22.

Sluming, V., Brooks, J., Howard, M., Downes, J.J., and Roberts, N. (2007) 'Broca's area supports enhanced visuospatial cognition in orchestral musicians.' *Journal of Neuroscience*, 27 (14), 3799–806.

Smith, A. (2000) *Researching Quality of Life of Older People: Concepts, measures and findings (Working paper no.7)*. Keele: Centre for Social Gerontology, Keele University.

Smith, J., and Freund, A.M. (2002) 'The dynamics of possible selves in old age'. *The Journals of Gerontology Series B: Psychological Sciences and Social Sciences*, 57 (6), 492–500.

Smith, K.P., and Christakis, N.A. (2008) 'Social networks and health'. *Annual Review of Sociology*, 34 (1), 405–29.

Sokolov, E.N. (1963) 'Higher nervous functions: the orienting reflex'. *Annual Review of Physiology*, 25 (March), 545–80.

Southcott, J. E. (2009) 'And as I go, I love to sing: The Happy Wanderers, music and positive aging'. *International Journal of Community Music*, 2 (2/3), 143–56.

Spigner-Littles, D., and Anderson, C.E. (1999) 'Constructivism: A paradigm for older learners'. *Educational Gerontology*, 25 (3), 203–9.

Spintge, R. (2012) 'Clinical use of music in Operating Theatre'. In MacDonald, R., Kreutz, G., and Mitchell, L. (eds) *Music, Health and Wellbeing*, 276–88. Oxford: Oxford University Press.

Spintge, R., and Droh, R. (1992) *MusikMedizen: Physiologische Grundlagen und praktische*. Anwendungen. Stuttgart: Fischer.

Springate, I., Atkinson, M., and Martin, K. (2008) *Intergenerational Practice: a review of the literature*. LGA Research Report F/SR262, Slough: NFER.

Stacey, R., Brittain, K., and Kerr, S. (2002) 'Singing for health: An exploration of the issues'. *Health Education*, 102 (4), 156–62.

Steptoe, A. (1997) 'Stress and disease'. In Baum, A., Newman, A., Weinman, J., West, R., and McManus, C. (eds) *Cambridge Handbook of Psychology, Health, and Medicine*. Cambridge: Cambridge University Press, 174–7.

Steverink, N., and Lindenberg, S. (2006) 'Which social needs are important for subjective well-being? What happens to them with ageing?' *Psychology and Ageing*, 21, 281–90.

Stige, B. (2010) 'Practicing music as mutual care'. In Stige, B., Ansell, G., Elefant, C., and Pavlicevic, M. (eds) *Where Music Helps. Community Music Therapy in Action and Reflection*. Farnham: Ashgate, 253–75.

Strange, C.C., and Banning, J.H. (2001) *Educating by Design*. San Francisco: Jossey-Bass.

Stuart-Hamilton, I. (2006) *The Psychology of Ageing: An introduction*. 4th ed. London: Jessica Kingsely.

Suzuki, M., Kanamori, M., Nagasawa, S., Tokiko, L., and Takayuki, S. (2007) 'Music therapy-induced changes in behavioural evaluations, and saliva chromogranin A and immunoglobulin A concentrations in elderly patients with senile dementia'. *Geriatrics and Gerontology International*, 7 (1), 61–71.

Suzuki, M., Kanamori, M., Watanabe, M., Nagasawa, S. Kojima, O., and Nakahara, D. (2004) 'Behavioural and endocrinological evaluation of music therapy for elderly patients with dementia', *Nursing and Health Sciences*, 6 (1), 11–18.

Svansdottir, H.B., and Snaedal, J. (2006) 'Music therapy in moderate and severe dementia of Alzheimer's type: a case-control study'. *International Psychogeriatrics*, 18 (4), 613–21.

Takahashi, T., and Matsushita, H. (2006) 'Long-term effects of music therapy on elderly with moderate/severe dementia'. *Journal of Music Therapy,* 43 (4), 317–33.

Taylor, A., and Hallam, S. (2008) 'Understanding what it means for older students to learn basic musical skills on a keyboard instrument'. *Music Education Research,* 10 (2), 285–306.

Tesch-Römer, C., and Wurm, S. (2012) 'Research on active aging in Germany'. *The Journal of Gerontopsychology and Geriatric Psychiatry,* 25 (3), 167–70.

Thaut, M.H. (2005) *Rhythm, Music and the Brain.* London: Taylor and Francis.

Thaut, M.H., McIntosh, K.H., McIntosh, G.C., and Hoemberg, V. (2001) 'Auditory rhythmicity enhances movement and speech motor control in patients with Parkinson's disease'. *Functional Neurology,* XVI (2), 163–72.

Thaut, M.H., Peterson, D.A., and McIntosh, G.C. (2005) 'Temporal entrainment of cognitive functions: Musical mnemonics induce brain plasticity and oscillatory synchrony in neural networks underlying memory'. *Annals of the New York Academy of Sciences,* 1060, 243–54.

Thomése, F., Van Tilburg, T., Broese van Groenou, M., and Knipscheer, K. (2005) 'Network dynamics in later life'. In Johnson, M.L. (ed.) *The Cambridge Handbook of Age and Ageing.* New York: Cambridge University Press, 463–68.

Trondalen, G., and Bonde, L.O. (2012) 'Music therapy: Models and interventions'. In MacDonald, R., Kreutz, G., and Mitchell, L. (eds) *Music, Health and Wellbeing.* Oxford: Oxford University Press, 40–62.

Tsugawa, S. (2008) *Senior Adult Music Learning and Participation: A review of the pertinent research literature.* Version 21. Online. http://sundevilsam.blogspot. co.uk/ (accessed 17 August 2013).

UK Office for National Statistics (2010) *Standard Occupational Classification.* Online. www.ons.gov.uk/ons/guide–method/classifications/current–standard–classifications/soc2010/index.html (accessed 7 August 2012).

UNESCO (2010) *Seoul Agenda: Goals for the development of arts education.* Seoul: United Nations Educational, Scientific and Cultural Organization. Online. http:// tinyurl.com/nn4pt5v (accessed 4 July 2013).

United Nations (2013) *World Population Prospects: The 2012 revision, key findings and advance tables.* New York: United Nations Department of Economic and Social Affairs/Population Division. Working Paper No. ESA/P/WP.227. Online. http://tinyurl.com/owo2gbj (accessed 13 August 2013).

van Eck, M., Berkhof, H., Nicolson, N., and Sulon, J. (1996) 'The effects of perceived stress, traits, mood states, and stressful events on salivary cortisol'. *Psychosomatic Medicine,* 58 (5), 447–58.

VanderArk, S., Newman, I., and Bell, S. (1983) 'The effects of music participation on quality of life of the elderly'. *Music Therapy,* 3 (1), 71–81.

Varvarigou, M., Creech, A., Hallam, S., and McQueen, H. (2012a) 'Benefits experienced by older people in group music-making activities'. *Journal of Applied Arts and Health,* 3 (2), 183–98.

— (2012b) 'Bringing different generations together in music-making – an intergenerational music project in east London'. *International Journal of Community Music,* 4 (3), 207–20.

Varvarigou, M., Hallam, S., Creech, A. and McQueen, H. (2013) 'Different ways of experiencing music-making in later life: Creative music sessions for older learners in east London'. *Research Studies in Music Education*, 35 (1), 103–18.

Vella-Burrows, T. (2012) *Singing and People with Dementia*. Canterbury: Canterbury Christ Church University.

Vella-Burrows, T., and Hancox, G. (2012) *Singing and People with Parkinson's*. Canterbury Christ Church University, Canterbury.

Verghese, J., Lipton, R.B., Katz, M.J., Hall, C.B., Derby, C.A., Kuslansky, G., Ambrose, A.F., Sliwinski, M., and Buschke, H. (2003) 'Leisure activities and the risk of dementia in the elderly'. *New England Journal of Medicine*, 348 (25), 2508–16. Online. www.nejm.org/doi/full/10.1056/NEJMoa022252 (accessed 6 September 2013).

Villar, F., Celdrán, M., Pinazo, S., and Triadó, C. (2010) 'The teacher's perspective in older education: The experience of teaching in a university for older people in Spain'. *Educational Gerontology*, 36 (10), 951–67.

Vollert, J.O., Stork, T., Rose, M., and Mockel, M. (2003) 'Musik als begleitende Therapie bei koronarer Herzkrankheit'. *Deutsche Medizinische Wochenschrift*, 128, 2712–16.

Waldemar G., Dubois, B., Emre, M., Georges, J., McKeith, I.G., Rossor, M., Scheltens, P., Tariska, P., and Winblad, B. (2007) 'Recommendations for the Diagnosis and Management of Alzheimer's Disease and Other Disorders Associated with Dementia: EFNS Guideline'. *European Journal of Neurology*, 14 (1) 1–26.

Walker, A., (2008) 'Commentary: The emergence and application of active aging in Europe'. *Journal of Aging & Social Policy*, 21 (1), 75–93.

Wallin, N., Merker, B., and Brown, S. (2000) *The Origins of Music*. Cambridge, MA: The MIT Press.

Weiss, R.S., and Bass, S.A. (eds) (2002) *Challenges of the Third Age: Meaning and purpose in later life*. New York: Oxford University Press.

West, S. (2003) 'Mining Tin Pan Alley: The songs of Tin Pan Alley as a social, musical and educational resource in the development of music making based on a community-focused social/altruistic philosophy'. *Youth Studies Australia*, 22 (2), 25–31. Online. http://tinyurl.com/oktlvhu (accessed 6 September 2013).

WHO (2002) *Active Ageing: A policy framework*. Geneva, Switzerland: World Health Organization. Online. http://whqlibdoc.who.int/hq/2002/who_nmh_nph_02.8.pdf (accessed 15 August 2013).

Wiggins, R.D., Netuveli, G., Hyde, E.M., Higgs, E.P., and Blane, E.D. (2007) 'The development and assessment of a quality of life measure (CASP–19) in the context of research on ageing'. Online. http://eprints.ioe.ac.uk/3286/1/Wiggins2008theevaluation61.pdf (accessed 26 September 2013).

Wise, G.W., Hartmann, D.J., and Fisher, B.J. (1992) 'Exploration of the relationship between choral singing and successful aging', *Psychological Reports*, 70, 1175–83.

Withnall, A. (2010) *Improving Learning in Later Life*. Abingdon, Oxon: Routledge.

Withnall, A, and Percy, K. (1994) *Good Practice in the Education and Training of Older Adults*. Aldershot, England: Ashgate.

Withnall, A., McGivney, V., and Soulsby, J. (2004) *Older People Learning: Myths and realities*. Leicester: NIACE with the UK Department for Education and Skills.

Wood, A. (2010) 'Singing diplomats: The hidden life of a Russian-speaking choir in Jerusalem'. *Ethnomusicology Forum*, 19 (2), 165–9.

Wood, E., Lanuza, C., Baciu, I., MacKenzie, M., and Nosko, A. (2010) 'Instructional styles, attitudes and experiences of seniors in computer workshops'. *Educational Gerontology*, 36 (10), 834–57.

Yong, E. (2009) 'Secrets of the centenarians: Life begins at 100'. *New Scientist*, 2724 (7 September). Online. www.newscientist.com/article/mg20327241.300-secrets-of-the-centenarians-life-begins-at-100.html?full=true (requires subscription).

Zanini, C.R., and Leao, E.T. (2006) 'Therapeutic choir: A music therapist looks at the new millennium elderly'. *Voices: A World Forum for Music Therapy*, 6 (2). Online. https://normt.uib.no/index.php/voices/article/viewArticle/249/193 (accessed 24 August 2013).

Zatorre, R.J., Perry, D.W., Beckett, C.A., Westbury, C.F., and Evans, A.C. (1998) 'Functional anatomy of musical processing in listeners with absolute pitch and relative pitch'. *Proceedings of the National Academy of Sciences of the United States of America*, 95 (6), 3172–7.

Zendel, B.R., and Alain, C. (2012) 'Musicians experience less age-related decline in central auditory processing'. *Psychology and Aging*, 27 (2), 410–17.

— (2013) 'The influence of lifelong musicianship on neurophysiological measures of concurrent sound segregation'. *Journal of Cognitive Neuroscience*, 25 (4), 503–16.

Index